EXTRA LIFE

The Astonishing Story of How We Doubled Our Lifespan

STEVEN JOHNSON

VIKING

VIKING

An imprint of Penguin Random House LLC, New York

First published in the United States of America by Viking,
an imprint of Penguin Random House LLC, 2023

Visit us online at penguinrandomhouse.com.

LIBRARY OF CONGRESS CATALOGING-IN-PUBLICATION DATA

Names: Johnson, Steven, 1968– author. Title: Extra life : the astonishing story of how we doubled our lifespan / Steven Johnson. Description: New York : Viking, an imprint of Penguin Random House LLC, 2023. | Includes bibliographical references and index. | Audience: Ages 8–12 | Audience: Grades 4–6 | Summary: "Humans live longer now than they ever have in their more than three hundred thousand years of existence on earth. And most (if not all) of the advances that have permitted the human lifespan to double have happened in living memory. *Extra Life* looks at vaccines, seat belts, pesticides, and more, and how each of our scientific advancements have prolonged human life. This book is a deep dive into the sciences—perfect for younger readers who enjoy modern history as well as scientific advances"—Provided by publisher. Identifiers: LCCN 2022021894 (print) | LCCN 2022021895 (ebook) | ISBN 9780593351499 (hardcover) | ISBN 9780593351505 (ebook) Subjects: LCSH: Health expectancy—History—Juvenile literature. | Medical care—History—Juvenile literature. | Life expectancy—History—Juvenile literature. | Medical sciences—History—Juvenile literature. | Technology—History—Juvenile literature. Classification: LCC RA418 .J588 2023 (print) | LCC RA418 (ebook) | DDC 614.4/2—dc23 /eng/20220617 LC record available at https://lccn.loc.gov/2022021894 LC ebook record available at htps://lccn.loc.gov/2022021895

Printed in the United States of America

ISBN 9780593351499

1st Printing

LBC

Edited by Ken Wright and Catherine Frank
Design by Monique Sterling
Text set in Plantin

For my mother

CONTENTS

INTRODUCTION

It may not feel like it if you check the news, but you are living in a world that is far safer than the one in which your great-great-grandparents lived. Countless everyday experiences that used to pose terrible threats to our lives now pose no meaningful health risk at all. That glass of milk you had with dinner last night? A little more than a century ago, it might have contained germs that could cause the deadly disease tuberculosis. The scrape on your knee from falling off your longboard? That might have triggered a fatal infection just eighty years ago. Driving a car is ten times safer than it was when people first got behind the wheel.

There are a thousand other improvements in health and safety like these, but they all add up to one amazing statistic, maybe the most important statistic of all. It's what we call *life expectancy*: the number of years that the average person born at a given place and time can expect to live. Take a look at this chart of life expectancy in the United Kingdom, where they have been measuring it the longest:

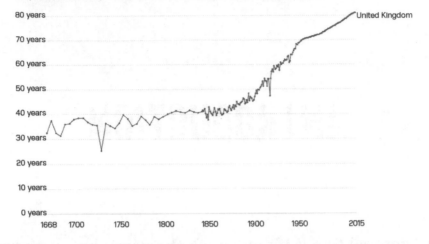

LIFE EXPECTANCY

Shown is a period life expectancy at birth, the average number of years a newborn would live if the pattern of mortality in the given year were to stay the same throughout its life.

The average person born in the United States a century ago could expect to live a little more than forty years. Today that number is just below eighty years. And Americans are four times more likely to live into their hundreds than they were a few decades ago. It's an incredible transformation, and it's not just happening in wealthy countries like the United States or the United Kingdom. A hundred years ago, life expectancy in India was only twenty-five years. Now it's seventy years. As a species, it's as though we've been given an entire extra life to live, compared to our ancestors.

Some of that extra life is the result of elderly people living longer. Think about your own extended family. Many of us have grandparents or great-grandparents who are in their eighties or nineties. Living that long is normal now. But it didn't used to be.

Another major factor in the story of life expectancy is how it changed what it means to be a child. For most of human history, about a third of all children died before they turned eighteen. Today it's closer to one in a hundred.

So why isn't the story of extended life something we hear about all the time? Why isn't it front page news? Because, most of the time, it doesn't involve the sudden, dramatic changes that draw media attention. The changes that made our world so much safer were subtle, incremental ones. They were slow and steady. In the long run, they add up to the most momentous transformation you could imagine. But in the short run, they are often invisible.

One of the reasons we have a hard time recognizing this kind of progress is that, by definition, it is measured in nonevents: the smallpox infection that didn't kill you at age two, the lead paint that didn't give you brain damage, the drinking water that didn't poison you with cholera. We don't tend to think about these kinds of things for a good reason: they didn't happen! But they might well have happened if you or I had been born just two centuries ago, even in the wealthiest countries in the world.

Think about it this way: We build monuments and pay tribute to the lives lost in wars or great tragedies, and that makes sense. But we don't have a habit of building monuments that celebrate deaths that didn't happen, monuments to all the lives saved. Maybe it's time we did.

In a sense, human beings have been increasingly protected by an invisible shield, one that has been built, piece by piece, over the last few centuries, keeping us ever safer and further from death. It protects us through countless interventions, big and small: the chlorine in our drinking water, the vaccinations that rid the world of smallpox, the data centers mapping disease outbreaks all around the planet.

A crisis like the global pandemic that began in 2020 gives us a new perspective on all that progress. Pandemics have an interesting tendency to make that invisible shield suddenly and briefly visible. For once, we're reminded of how dependent everyday life is on medical science, hospitals, public health authorities, drug supply chains, and more. And an event like the COVID-19 crisis does something else as well: it helps us perceive the holes in that shield, the vulnerabilities, the places where we need new scientific breakthroughs, new systems, new ways of protecting ourselves from emergent threats.

Most history books focus on a central topic: a person, event, or place, a great leader, a military conflict, a city, or a nation. This book, by contrast, tells the story of a number: the rising life expectancy of the world's population, giving us an entire extra life in merely one century. It should help you understand where that progress came from, the breakthroughs and collaborations and institutions that had to be invented to make it possible.

Some of the heroes of this story were scientists or doctors, but not all. Some of them were ordinary people who fought to improve the health of our species by writing articles or organizing protests or sharing an important breakthrough they had discovered in another culture. But they were all people who had a vision of how the world could be made a better place and who had the daring and the commitment to turn that vision into a reality. This book tells the story of how they pulled it off.

CHAPTER ONE

THE·SPECKLED·MONSTER
(Vaccines)

If you had been born three centuries ago, the list of potential illnesses or accidents that could threaten your life would be very different from that list today. You would be at no risk from automobile or plane crashes or from being accidentally electrocuted because none of those technologies existed in the early 1700s. That would be the good news. But for the most part, the list of potential threats would be much longer than it is now. Getting a simple cut or scrape—the sort of thing that you'd put a Band-Aid on now and forget about—could easily lead to a deadly infection back then. The simple act of drinking water—particularly in big towns and cities—could give you a disease like typhoid.

But for many people in the early 1700s, the most terrifying threat they faced was a virus. Scientists later gave it the name *variola major*, when they finally identified it in microscopes a century and a half later. The disease it caused went by another name: smallpox.

Smallpox had been a scourge since at least the age of the great Egyptian pyramids. (The mummy of Ramses V has visible scars on his face from the pustules that form on the skin of smallpox victims.) In some European cities between 1650 and 1750, smallpox accounted for more than 15 percent of all deaths recorded. Young children were particularly vulnerable to the disease. In Sweden during the eighteenth century, 90 percent of smallpox deaths occurred in children under the age of ten. Parents lived with the knowledge that at any moment their child could come down with a fever, followed by the telltale rash, and within a matter of days, the child would be dead—often followed in short order by their siblings. Compared to our modern experience, the whole notion of childhood was inverted. Today we think of children as emblems of vitality and resilience, the vigor of youth. But in the age of smallpox, childhood was fundamentally linked to sudden and catastrophic illness. Being a child in 1700 was *dangerous*.

No amount of wealth or education could protect you from the "speckled monster," as smallpox was sometimes called. The list of European leaders felled by smallpox between 1600 and 1800 staggers the mind. During the outbreak of 1711 alone, smallpox killed Holy Roman Emperor Joseph I, three siblings of the future Holy Roman Emperor Francis I, and the heir to the French throne, the Grand Dauphin Louis. Over the next seventy years, the disease claimed King Louis I of Spain, Emperor Peter II of Russia, Louise Hippolyte, Princess of Monaco, King Louis XV of France, and Maximilian III Joseph, Elector of Bavaria. These were some of the richest people in the world, living in vast palaces with access to the finest health care of the day, and they were just as likely to succumb to smallpox as a common laborer. Smallpox was an equal opportunity killer.

It's no accident, then, that one of the first major breakthroughs in the history of medicine was a response to the speckled monster. It's a famous story, famous enough to sometimes appear in history books that don't usually give enough attention to advances in human health.

The story goes like this: In the late 1790s, an English doctor named Edward Jenner observed a strange pattern in the smallpox cases he was seeing in the rural community where he practiced. Milkmaids seemed less likely than the average resident to contract smallpox. You could see the difference in their faces—very few of the milkmaids had the telltale scarring of a smallpox survivor. Like a good medical detective, Jenner realized that this pattern was a clue. He began developing an idea that the milkmaids had been exposed to another virus known as cowpox—a less deadly cousin of *variola major*—thanks to all the time they spent milking cows.

The milkmaids' unblemished skin gave Jenner an idea: maybe contracting cowpox somehow *protected* them from smallpox. And so Jenner decided to deliberately infect one of his patients with cowpox to see if his theory was right. On the May 14, 1796, Jenner performed his now legendary experiment.

He scraped some pus from the cowpox blisters of a milkmaid and inserted the material into the arms of an eight-year-old boy. The boy developed a light fever but soon proved to be immune from smallpox. According to most medical histories, it was a milestone in the history of medicine: a "eureka moment" that led to the world's first vaccine, the beginning of a medical revolution that would save countless lives over the subsequent centuries.

Jenner is undoubtedly a hero. But the real story behind the smallpox vaccine is more complex—and more surprising—than the conventional version of Jenner's eureka moment. This story has another, more unlikely hero—or heroine, as it happens: a brilliant young woman with no medical training who moved from London to Istanbul as a young mother, a move that ultimately changed the world.

Mary Montagu

Born in 1689, Lady Mary Montagu was the daughter of the Duke of Kingston-upon-Hull and wife of the grandson of the Earl of Sandwich. She was brilliant, witty, and beautiful. As a teenager, she had written novellas; in her early twenties, she struck up a correspondence with the poet Alexander Pope. At the age of twenty-five, she contracted smallpox and nearly died. Despite the fact that she had access to the very finest doctors of the age, the treatments prescribed to her make it clear how pathetic medicine was in the early 1700s: The physicians drained blood from her body and gave her poisons that made her throw up. She received a regular dose of a medicine that included saltpeter—the key ingredient in gunpowder. The doctors prescribed beer and wine as her primary beverages during her illness.

Somehow she survived, and shortly thereafter, her husband, Edward Worley Montagu, was appointed Ambassador to the Ottoman Empire, which was based in the country we now call Turkey. In 1716, after spending her entire life in London and the English countryside, Mary Montagu moved her growing family to Constantinople (now called Istanbul), living there for two years.

Montagu immersed herself in the culture of the city, visiting the legendary baths and learning Turkish in order to read the country's poets in their original tongue. She studied Turkish cooking and began dressing in the style of Turkish women, concealing her smallpox scars behind veils. She had an unusual interest in the conventions of this very different culture, and that innate sense of curiosity led to a crucial breakthrough in the story of life expectancy. In one of her letters back to her friends in England, she took note of a strange custom she had observed during her stay: a "set of old women" who would come to people's houses with a nutshell full of pus from smallpox victims and deliberately expose children to the virus.

Montagu called this procedure *engrafting*, but it is now generally known by another name: *variolation*. (It's also sometimes called *inoculation*.) No one knows exactly when and where variolation was first practiced. Some accounts suggest it may have originated in the Indian subcontinent thousands of years ago. One historian describes a "hermit" from the Szechuan Province in southwest China who brought the technique to the royal court of Wang Tang after the Chinese minister's son died of smallpox. Whatever its origins, the historical record is clear that the practice had spread throughout China, India, and Persia by the 1600s. Like many great ideas in history, it may have been independently discovered multiple times in unconnected regions of the world.

In one fundamental sense, variolation is similar to the vaccination technique that Edward Jenner would invent eighty years after Mary Montagu first observed it. Neither Montagu nor Jenner understood anything about viruses and the immune system, but in modern scientific language we can describe why both procedures worked: They took a small amount of the virus that causes a disease and injected it into a person's bloodstream, just enough to train that person's immune system to recognize and attack that virus, but not enough to make them critically ill with the disease. That exposure gave the person immunity to the virus, which then protected them against future encounters with *variola major*.

There was a difference between the two approaches, however. Jenner's vaccine used the cowpox virus, not the smallpox virus. Because the two viruses were close relatives, an immune system trained to recognize cowpox was then prepared to fight off its more dangerous cousin. The variolation procedure that Montagu discovered in Turkey used samples of the actual smallpox virus to create immunity. And that made it much riskier. There was about a 2 percent chance of dying from variolation and a much higher chance that you would get quite sick after the procedure. Jenner's approach was about ten times safer, which is why it was such a breakthrough. (Modern vaccines use more advanced approaches—dead or genetically modified viruses—which make them even more safe than Jenner's technique.) But overall, variolation and vaccination were achieving the same goal through similar means.

Montagu was so impressed with the procedure that she took a courageous step. She decided to engraft her own son. On March 23, 1718, she sent a brief note to her husband that announced: "The Boy was engrafted last Tuesday and is at this time singing and playing, and very impatient for his supper. I pray God my next may give as good an account of him." After a few days of fever and an outbreak of pustules on both arms, Montagu's son made a full recovery. He would go on to live into his sixties, seemingly immune to smallpox for the rest of his life. He is considered the first British citizen to have undergone variolation. His sister, who was successfully engrafted in 1721 after Montagu and her family had returned to London, was the first person to undergo the procedure on British soil.

Word spread quickly through the drawing rooms and palaces of aristocratic England: Mary Montagu had brought back a miracle cure from Turkey, one that finally promised an effective shield against the most terrifying threat of the era. In late 1722, the princess of Wales inoculated two of her children, including her son Frederick, the heir to the British throne. Frederick would survive his childhood untouched by smallpox, and while he died before ascending to the throne, he did live long enough to produce an heir: George William Frederick, who would eventually become King George III.

The royal inoculations proved to be a tipping point. Thanks in large part to Mary Montagu's original advocacy, variolation spread through the wealthiest members of British society over the subsequent decades. It even spread to less well-born members of society. One of them was Edward Jenner himself.

Jenner had been inoculated as a young child in 1757, and in his capacity as a local doctor, he regularly inoculated his patients. This is why Mary Montagu—and all the unknown pioneers who developed variolation over the centuries before her—deserve recognition in the story. Without a life-long familiarity with variolation, it is unlikely that Jenner would have hit upon the idea of injecting someone with a less deadly but related virus.

The long-term impact of that idea turned out to be truly immense. Over the next two centuries, a long list of vaccines targeting other diseases— diphtheria, typhoid, polio, all the way to COVID-19—were created. The best estimates hold that more than a billion lives have been saved thanks to the invention and mass adoption of vaccination over that period.

So if you ask the question of where vaccines came from, there are really two ways of answering it. On the one hand, we have the satisfying narrative of brilliant Edward Jenner, inventing vaccination on one day in 1796. On the other, we have a much more complicated story, where part of an idea emerges halfway around the world and migrates from culture to culture through word of mouth, until a perceptive and influential young woman takes note of it and imports it to her home country, where it slowly begins to take root, ultimately allowing a country doctor to make a key improvement on the technique after decades of using it on his own patients.

The difference between the two explanations is the difference between the "lone genius" model of progress and the "collaborative network" model. Lone genius stories are a lot simpler to tell, but they rarely give us an accurate account of how important new breakthroughs develop and spread. And there are few breakthroughs more important in the history of our health than the invention of vaccines.

As we will see, Montagu's story is typical in another way. If you look at the history of extending life through the collaborative network lens, you'll find that people trained as scientists and physicians are only part of the network that drives meaningful change. Sometimes people like Mary Montagu— who was not a scientist or a doctor, just an observant and engaged woman with powerful connections—can play a pivotal role as well. They help spread the word of promising new solutions. Important breakthroughs in health don't just have to be invented. They also have to be argued for, championed, defended. It's true that new innovations in health need smart people to think of them. But we also need people to fight for those ideas.

CHAPTER TWO

THE·DETECTIVES
(Public Health Data)

One of the quiet miracles of modern life that rarely gets the appreciation it deserves is the abundance of clean drinking water in large towns and cities. Clean water is now commonplace in all but the poorest countries. Just a century and a half ago, most people in the world did not have running water in their homes. If they wanted water for drinking or cooking or bathing, they had to leave their homes and collect it from some kind of public supply: usually a pump connected to a well. That was challenging enough compared to just turning on a faucet in the kitchen sink. But the real problem with the water supply back then, particularly in big cities, was the fact that it could kill you.

One of the deadliest killers in the nineteenth century was a waterborne disease called cholera, which caused a catastrophic loss of bodily fluids, mostly through diarrhea. You could drink a glass of water contaminated by the bacterium that causes cholera and be dead in forty-eight hours. But because that bacterium was invisible to the human eye—scientists wouldn't detect it with microscopes until the 1870s—doctors and health officials didn't realize that people were getting sick from drinking water. Instead, they believed that diseases like cholera were transmitted by poisoned air and bad smells. This was known as the miasma theory of disease. Cities back then were indeed very smelly places, but the smells weren't causing people to die. Invisible microbes in their drinking water were the real culprit.

The way we finally figured out that cholera was caused by contaminated water is one of the great detective stories of medical history. In late August of 1854, a terrible outbreak of cholera erupted in the London neighborhood of Soho, which was, at the time, one of the poorest and most densely populated areas in the city. Within a few weeks, 10 percent of the neighborhood had died. Imagine how terrifying it must have been to walk through the streets of Soho during that period, seeing the bodies being piled up on carts to be taken to the morgue, knowing that some invisible killer was still stalking the area. Most of us would probably have locked ourselves into our homes or fled the city in fear. But one resident of Soho took a courageous stand and began knocking on doors, asking people where they got their drinking water.

His name was John Snow. He was a local doctor from a working-class family who had built up a career both as a physician and a medical innovator. For more than four years, in his spare time, Snow had been developing a theory that cholera was a disease caused by very small organisms in drinking water and not conveyed through polluted air. He'd published papers on it and collected extensive evidence to support his idea. But authorities ignored him, even mocked him in a few instances. The miasma theory was too entrenched, and no one could see these tiny organisms that Snow believed existed.

William Farr

When cholera erupted in his community in the last week of August, Snow recognized immediately that the intense concentration of the outbreak suggested that there might be a single point source that was causing people to become sick. If he could track all the deaths to a single source of water, he might finally be able to convince the authorities that his theory was correct—and stop the outbreak before it killed even more of his neighbors.

In this investigation, he was assisted by the work of another pioneer of public health: a statistician named William Farr. He had come up with the idea of publishing detailed reports every two weeks that shared information about deaths in the city: the age, sex, address, and occupation of the deceased, along with the cause of death. Farr had believed that by making that data publicly available, important patterns in disease might be discovered, helping people prevent the spread of outbreaks. Farr was also the first person who noticed that disease outbreaks followed a mathematical curve, rising and falling in predictable patterns. When public health officials, in the spring of 2020, started talking about "flattening the curve" of COVID, they were using language—and a mathematical approach to fighting disease—that William Farr invented.

The public data that Farr had published gave Snow a wealth of information that helped him understand which members of the Soho community were being affected by the disease. But he also needed more direct sources of information. In an act of staggering bravery—given the deadly outbreak that was devastating the neighborhood—Snow began knocking on doors, interviewing local residents about where they collected their water and if anyone in their household had contracted cholera. When we think about the classic figure of the detective in nineteenth-century London, walking the streets in pursuit of a deadly killer, we naturally think of the fictional investigator Sherlock Holmes. But John Snow was the real thing, only the killer he was in pursuit of was a microbe, not a person.

Snow found an unlikely ally in a local priest named Henry Whitehead, who was highly respected in the neighborhood. Whitehead helped Snow with his interviews. While Snow is often described as the hero of the story, in many ways this was a team effort: Snow combined his own data with Whitehead's and augmented it all with the mortality reports that Farr had published. But it was Snow who had the brilliant idea to take all that data and project it onto a map, one of the most famous maps in history. It looked like this:

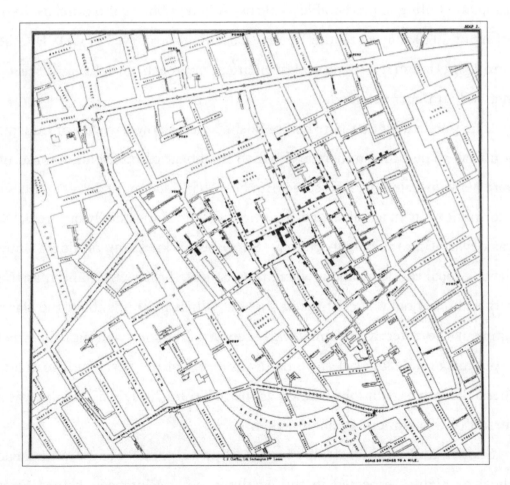

John Snow's map of the Soho outbreak

Each death in the neighborhood is marked with a little black bar. If only one person died at a specific address, Snow placed one black bar to represent that death at the appropriate place on the map. If five people died at the same address, Snow placed five black bars on the map.

When he finished putting all the data together, the map revealed a striking pattern: many of the deaths in the neighborhood were clustered around a popular pump at 40 Broad Street, one of the major sources of drinking water for all of Soho. The closer people lived to that one pump, the more likely they were to die. In other investigations, Snow showed that people who had contracted cholera who lived far from the pump had, for various reasons, decided to travel all the way to 40 Broad Street for their water.

Henry Whitehead contributed another critical piece of the puzzle. He identified what we now call the "patient zero" of the outbreak—the person who started the chain of infections. In the case of the Soho outbreak, it was a baby girl who lived next door to the pump on Broad Street, who had somehow contracted cholera a few days before the outbreak started. Because her family didn't have a toilet in the apartment—most people didn't back then—her parents had washed her messy diapers in the basement of their building. The basement was separated from the well by a thin wall of decaying bricks, which is how the cholera bacteria got into the well water and ultimately made the whole neighborhood sick.

Snow's map—and Whitehead's patient zero—turned out to make all the difference. When Snow shared the map with the authorities, they agreed to remove the handle of the Broad Street pump. That action was a milestone in the history of human health: the first official intervention based on the premise that drinking water was conveying deadly illness thanks to some kind of invisible agent in the water. It was the first serious blow to the miasma theory of disease.

Over the next few years, the medical establishment slowly embraced Snow's radical theory. In the late 1850s, London embarked on one of the most ambitious public works projects of the century: building a massive sewer system in order to separate out human waste from the city's drinking water. Overseen by a brilliant engineer named Joseph Bazalgette, the project took the entirely haphazard network of drainage and waste pipes that had been accumulating for centuries beneath the city's streets and replaced it with an organized system of sewer lines running eighty-two miles in total, using three hundred million bricks, including the massive interception lines that run along both banks of the River Thames, keeping the city's waste from flowing downhill into the river. (If you visit London and walk along the elevated embankments that run on both sides of the Thames, you are enjoying a structure built specifically to keep the city's drinking water free of cholera.) Amazingly, the main lines of the project were functional after only six years of work.

The project was a resounding success, and by 1866, London had virtually eradicated cholera from the city, little more than a decade after Snow had begun his investigation of the Soho outbreak.

The amazing thing about John Snow's triumph is that he was never able to see the deadly bacterium that caused such devastation in his neighborhood. He had spent hours in his home laboratory viewing samples of water from various sources through his microscope. But the lens-making technology of the age was not sufficiently advanced to allow him to perceive the organism that was causing the disease. (It would be another three decades before the German microbiologist Robert Koch identified the bacterium.) But Snow recognized that there were other ways of seeing, other ways of understanding and preventing the threat. What Snow couldn't do with microscopes, he was able to do with *data*, seeing the killer microbe indirectly in the pattern of deaths revealed by his map.

At some point during their investigations in the streets of Soho, Snow turned to Whitehead and remarked: "You and I may not live to see the day and my name will be forgotten when it comes; but the time will arrive when great outbreaks of cholera will be things of the past; and it is the knowledge of the way in which the disease is propagated which will cause them to disappear."

Snow was right about the decline of cholera epidemics, though he was wrong about his name being forgotten. Today in London there is replica of the pump—with a small plaque commemorating the breakthrough—standing on the sidewalk at what would have been 40 Broad Street, next to a corner pub that is now known as The John Snow. Public health workers make regular pilgrimages to the site; some sign a guestbook at the pub.

It's important that the city of London recognizes the contribution John Snow made back in 1854. But it's also striking how unusual that kind of memorial is. If you think about most large urban memorials, they're almost all devoted to military events and heroes: think of Lord Nelson towering above Trafalgar Square in London or the monument to Union soldiers in Grand Army Plaza in Brooklyn. But the John Snow pump is a rare exception: a memorial devoted to a public health breakthrough.

To be clear: the lives lost at the Battle of Trafalgar or during the Civil War deserve the memorials we have given them. But we should have more memorials like the Broad Street pump because they remind us of a different kind of history: a memorial to lives *saved*, to the millions of people around the world who didn't die of cholera, in part because a local physician in a poor neighborhood saw a pattern in the data and changed our understanding of how diseases spread.

CHAPTER THREE

MAPPING·THE·SEVENTH·WARD →
(Social Epidemiology)

In the twenty-first century, we have an understandable tendency to think about what keeps us healthy in terms of tangible innovations: vaccine injections that protect us from contagious diseases, medicines we take to fight off an infection, or high-tech scanners that detect cancerous growth in our bodies. But sometimes the innovations that really matter in keeping us alive don't come in the form of material objects. Sometimes the breakthrough is more abstract, as in the data revolution that John Snow helped create in the nineteenth century.

Data continues to be crucial to helping us live longer in the twenty-first century as well. Think about how important data was in the early days of the

COVID-19 pandemic. We didn't have vaccines or wonder drugs to keep us safe from the virus in those terrifying first months. Our best line of defense against the virus came from the data we used to track its spread. You may remember how everyone talked about flattening the curve by staying at home, wearing masks, or washing our hands. The reason we had a curve to flatten was because we were collecting data about COVID infections in communities all around the world, and that data let us see where the virus was rampant and where it was on the decline, which enabled us to adjust our behavior accordingly.

Data revealed something else important in the COVID pandemic: the disease had a disproportionate impact on communities of color. In New York, African Americans were twice as likely as white people to die from the disease. In Chicago, African Americans make up 29 percent of the population, but they accounted for 70 percent of the deaths related to COVID-19.

The idea of using data to track these inequalities dates back to the late 1800s and the work of the brilliant African American intellectual W. E. B. Du Bois. Where John Snow used data to show how invisible microbes in the water were killing people, Du Bois used similar techniques to explain how people's lives were being cut short by a different kind of threat, what we would now call *systemic racism*.

Today, Du Bois is best known as a civil rights activist and the author of the classic book *The Souls of Black Folk*. But Du Bois's career began with a study of a Black neighborhood in Philadelphia, published in 1899 in book form as *The Philadelphia Negro*. It was one of those books that made a whole new kind of thinking possible. Du Bois was the first to prove a troubling fact that has continued to haunt the United States in the age of COVID-19: African Americans were dying at higher rates than their white counterparts, and that tragic difference in life expectancy was partly caused by the oppressive forces of racism.

W. E. B. Du Bois

Du Bois was in his late twenties when he arrived in Philadelphia in 1896. He had just completed his PhD at Harvard—the first African American to do so—and had spent a heady two years in Europe studying sociology and philosophy at the University of Berlin. Du Bois's early success in the academic world was even more impressive given the deep-seated prejudice of the period. A number of books published by well-respected scholars during the 1890s had attempted to explain problems of crime and poverty in African American communities—what was then commonly called "the Negro problem"—with openly racist explanations, all revolving around traits that were seen as essential deficiencies of Black people. The books had titles like *Race Traits and Tendencies of the American Negro*.

Du Bois got a lucky break in 1896, when a group of Philadelphia citizens who were concerned about the rising crime and poverty in the city's African American neighborhoods decided to hire him to study the community, arranging a one-year post at the University of Pennsylvania. And so, in the summer of 1896, Du Bois and his wife moved into a one-room apartment at 700 Lombard Street on the eastern edge of an area known as the Seventh Ward, Philadelphia's largest African American neighborhood.

Du Bois understood that "the Negro problem" was not something internal to African Americans, but instead belonged to society itself. And he realized that part of that problem had to do with health. Everything about life gets more challenging when you are constantly battling illness or your children are at risk of an early death. The question was how to explain the challenges to the wider community.

Du Bois went into the project well aware that his sponsors still clung to racist beliefs about the core nature of the problem. Du Bois described their attitude as: "Something is wrong with a race that is responsible for so much crime." And so the young scholar decided to combat that prejudice with an amazing display of detective work, an even more comprehensive study of the neighborhood than the one John Snow had conducted in Soho forty years before.

"The problem lay before me," he would later write. "I studied it personally and not just by proxy. I sent out no canvassers. I went myself . . . I went through the Philadelphia libraries for data, gained access in many instances to private libraries of colored folk . . . I mapped the district, classifying it by conditions." For months, Du Bois would leave 700 Lombard each morning, with his trademark cane and gloves, and commence an eight-hour exploration of the Seventh Ward, knocking on doors, interviewing residents about their work lives and families, inspecting the conditions of their residences. By the end of the survey, Du Bois had spent more than eight hundred hours documenting the conditions of the neighborhood, visiting more than two thousand households in just three months of research. Some of the data he tabulated from the investigation would later be presented, like Snow had before, in the form of a map, each parcel in the ward color-coded to denote five classes of occupants: what Du Bois called "the vicious and criminal classes," "the poor," "the working people," "the middle classes," and the residences belonging to whites or commercial enterprises.

Du Bois assembled massive amounts of data about the health of the Seventh Ward, laying out the statistical evidence for the higher mortality rates of African Americans through more than a dozen charts and tables. On average, Black people were dying at a rate about 5 percent higher than their white neighbors. And while Du Bois never calculated life expectancy rates for the community, he did include several charts in the style of Farr's life tables that showed a shocking gap between Black and white families in terms of childhood mortality. Black Philadelphians were twice as likely as their white neighbors to die before the age of fifteen.

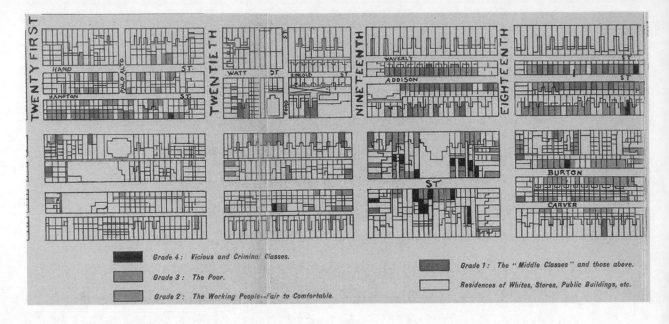

Grade 4 : *Vicious and Criminal Classes.*

Grade 3 : *The Poor.*

Grade 2 : *The Working People--Fair to Comfortable.*

Grade 1 : *The "Middle Classes" and those above.*

Residences of Whites, Stores, Public Buildings, etc.

Du Bois's map of Philadelphia's Seventh Ward

But Du Bois knew he had to do more than just document the difference, given the racial prejudices of the day. More importantly, he had to *explain* the difference, to prove that it was not just an inevitable consequence of the Seventh Ward being populated by an "inferior species." And so Du Bois used his skills as a data detective to document how the living conditions in the neighborhood were shortening the lives of its residents.

There were more than two thousand families living in the Seventh Ward, according to Du Bois's analysis, but only about three hundred of them had working toilets, and many of those families shared their toilets with other families in the same building. Many of them had no connection to running water. Many of the residences were overcrowded as well. In his survey, he documented two apartments where ten people shared a single room, and more than a hundred cases where apartments were occupied at a rate of four or more people per room.

Du Bois assembled this evidence to make a powerful point: people were dying in the Seventh Ward because they were crowded together in unsanitary conditions, a perfect breeding environment for diseases like tuberculosis. But Du Bois went even further in his analysis. African Americans were living in such unhealthy environments because of the wider problem of prejudice in the city. "The undeniable fact that most Philadelphia white people prefer not to live near Negroes limits the Negro very seriously in his choice of a home and especially in the choice of a cheap home," he wrote. While working-class whites often found jobs in factories outside the city center, which let them settle in less crowded residential areas, Du Bois pointed out that "the mass of Negroes are in the economic world purveyors to the rich— working in private houses, in hotels, large stores, etc. In order to keep this work they must live nearby . . . Thus it is clear that the nature of the Negro's work compels him to crowd into the center of the city much more than is the case with the mass of white working people."

In his analysis of the Seventh Ward, Du Bois invented a new way of understanding health inequalities using data: connecting the basic facts of mortality and illness (who died and who lived) with the physical environment that shaped those lives (how many toilets, how many residents per room) and then linking both those statistical surveys to broader societal forces. In a way, Du Bois was making an early, influential version of the argument that now goes by the slogan Black Lives Matter. His detective work explained that Black lives were being shortened by the way racism limited their options for sanitary housing.

The fact that so many African Americans were dying early from contagious diseases like tuberculosis was not the result of some inherent propensity for disease in the "Negro race," Du Bois made clear; it was the indirect consequence of the way society was organized to channel African Americans into the most unhealthy spaces in the entire city. It wasn't possible to solve the health crisis of the Seventh Ward by simply demanding that African Americans adopt healthier lifestyles; the entire system had to change to improve those health outcomes.

Like John Snow's detective work battling cholera, the innovations in data analysis that Du Bois introduced continue to play an essential role in our battle against twenty-first-century health threats. One of the main reasons that COVID-19 has been so much worse for Black and Latino citizens in the United States is the fact that those groups live, on average, in more crowded homes where viruses can easily spread, just like the residents of the Seventh Ward. In the past few years, a number of scientists have made breakthroughs in understanding how poverty and discrimination can cause long-term health problems, largely through the dangerous effects of chronic stress on the body. We haven't eliminated these problems yet, but thanks to the pioneering work of W. E. B. Du Bois, we can use data to identify and understand the problem, which is the first critical step to solving it.

CHAPTER FOUR

SAFE·AS·MILK
(Pasteurization)

July 4, 1850, was a scorchingly hot day in Washington, DC. On the site of what would become the Washington Monument, President Zachary Taylor gathered with a number of dignitaries in the blistering heat, participating in a fundraiser for the new monument. When the ceremonies finally came to an end, a dehydrated Taylor returned to the White House and gulped down a glass of ice-chilled milk.

Five days later, only sixteen months into his presidency, Taylor was dead, killed by a fast-moving digestive illness. Historians now believe that Taylor died because the milk he drank on the Fourth of July contained some kind of bacteria that replicated in his digestive tract.

It may seem strange to think of anyone—much less the president of the United States—being killed by a glass of milk, but in the nineteenth century, milk was a major health threat. And it was particularly dangerous for children. Even though the invention of vaccines had reduced the threat of smallpox, young people in the middle of the nineteenth century faced serious health challenges, and the problem had only grown worse in big cities. At the start of the century, in most large American cities, a quarter of all reported deaths involved children under the age of five, still a shocking number by modern standards. But by the 1840s, more than half of all deaths in New York were infants and young children. Some of those deaths were from the contaminated drinking water that John Snow battled against in London. But another major killer was milk.

Drinking animal milk—which humans have been doing for thousands of years—has always presented health risks, either through infections passed down from the animal itself or from spoilage. But crowded industrial-age cities like New York made the risks of drinking milk far worse. The island of Manhattan had a long tradition of dairy farmers, producing milk for New Yorkers clustered at the southern tip of the island on farms scattered across the still-rural areas in northern Manhattan and Brooklyn. But as the city swiftly colonized those regions during the nineteenth century, traditional farmland disappeared.

Remember that in the middle of the 1800s, there was no such thing as a refrigerator to keep milk and other food chilled. (Fridges wouldn't become common household appliances for almost a century.) Without refrigeration, milk would spoil in summer months if it was brought in from far-flung pastures in New Jersey or upstate New York. And so dairy producers realized they needed to figure out a way to maintain herds of cows *inside* the city limits. The problem was: How could you feed all that cattle without access to open, grassy pastures?

The dairy industry came up with a solution that, at first glance, seemed clever. They partnered with whiskey makers in the city, using one of the waste products from their alcohol production—sometimes called "slop" or "swill"—to feed the cows. Cows living off a diet of whiskey swill produced an unappetizing, blue-colored milk, but at least it could be delivered fresh to the exploding population of Manhattan.

Before long, whole neighborhoods of New York City were overrun with industrial dairy producers, with thousands of cows crowded into stalls, housed in fully urban neighborhoods in Manhattan and Brooklyn. The cows would be tied to a single stall for their entire lives, and boiling slop from the distilleries was poured into a trough in front of them. Feeding the cows exclusively swill gave them terrible sores and caused their tails to fall off. Many cows lost their teeth.

But as gruesome as the process was, it did manage to produce copious amounts of cheap milk, which the dairy producers mixed with chalk, flour, and eggs to make it look more like "Pure Country Milk"—the misleading branding they used to the describe the product. The combination of the advertising and the cheap prices—as little as six cents per quart—soon had the working classes of Manhattan and other cities around the country hooked on swill milk. And almost immediately, children began dying at a terrifying rate.

Political cartoon from 1872

How, then, did milk go from being "liquid poison"—as people started calling swill milk—to the much less dangerous drink we enjoy today?

The usual answer you will hear is that we made milk safe through chemistry—in particular, through the work of one man who is now so famous that his name is on just about every carton of milk in the grocery store today: Louis Pasteur. He was the French scientist famous for realizing that microbes, or *germs*, that were invisible to the naked eye were causing disease. Spoiled milk, Pasteur argued, was milk that had been colonized by tiny bacteria that were harmful to humans when you swallowed them. Those microbes were a danger in any unrefrigerated milk, but they were particularly dangerous when the milk had originated in the unsanitary swill milk facilities.

After a long series of experiments, mostly with wine, Pasteur determined that heating liquids to around 130 degrees Fahrenheit killed off those microbes, removing the threat. We now call that process *pasteurization*, and almost every brand of milk sold today is pasteurized.

But making milk safe wasn't just about chemistry experiments, and the easiest way to understand why is to look at the historical timeline. Pasteur invented his amazing technique in 1865. But pasteurized milk didn't become the standard until around 1920—half a century later!

Why did it take so long for such a good idea to take root? Because coming up with an important life-saving idea like pasteurization is only half of the problem. You also have to get that idea implemented; you have to persuade people that it's better than what they are used to. In the story of our extended life, those persuaders should be celebrated alongside the scientists like Pasteur, who traditionally get most of the glory.

And in the case of milk, one of the most important persuaders was an unlikely one: a man who made his money from selling luxury goods in department stores. His name was Nathan Straus.

Born in Bavaria, in what is now part of southeast Germany, in 1848, Nathan Straus moved at the age of eight with his family to the American South, where his father had established a profitable general store. The move turned out to have been disastrously timed. Pushed to the edges of poverty by the Civil War, the family relocated to New York just as Nathan was reaching adulthood. In Manhattan, the Straus family found their footing. Nathan began his career by working for his father's crockery and glassware firm; he and his brothers sold the pans and plates they manufactured to the new department stores that had exploded onto the commerce and fashion world in the 1870s. In early 1873, they began renting a space in the basement of Macy's flagship Fourteenth Street emporium to display their china, glass, and pottery. It soon became one of the most popular destinations in the store. A little more than a decade later, the Straus brothers had acquired Macy's outright.

Perhaps because of his family's own experience with sudden poverty when he was a boy, Nathan Straus spent a significant measure of his time and resources attempting to improve the conditions of New York City's homeless population and working poor. He opened shelters that housed more than fifty thousand people and distributed coal during the brutal winter and economic downturn of 1892–93. At one of their department stores, he built a cafeteria that offered a free meal plan for his employees, one of the first such programs ever created.

Nathan Straus

Straus had long been concerned about the childhood mortality rates in the city and had himself lost two children to disease. At some point in the late 1800s, he learned about pasteurization, which was finally being applied to milk, almost a quarter century after Pasteur himself had first developed it. Something about the process resonated with Straus, maybe because it was such a simple and effective means of keeping children alive.

Straus realized that solving the scientific problem of keeping milk safe was only the first step. He also had to change people's attitudes and behavior. In 1892, he created a milk laboratory where sterilized milk could be produced in large quantities. The next year, he began opening what he called "milk depots" in low-income neighborhoods around the city that sold milk to poor New Yorkers at extremely low prices. The first depot was located on a pier on the outer edges of the Lower East Side; records suggest that Straus dispensed 34,400 bottles of milk that first year.

Straus also did some important detective work in the style of John Snow and W. E. B. Du Bois. After being appointed health commissioner of the city in 1897, Straus learned that there had been terrible health problems in an orphanage situated on Randall's Island in the East River. In the preceding three years, 1,509 of the 3,900 children housed in the orphanage had died—a mortality rate even higher than the dismal rates in low-income communities around the city.

Like John Snow and the Broad Street pump, Straus suspected that the dairy herd that had been established on the island to supply the orphans with fresh milk was in fact the culprit. Straus funded a pasteurization plant on Randall's Island that supplied sterilized milk to the orphans. Nothing else in their diet or living conditions was altered. Almost immediately, the mortality rate dropped 14 percent. It was proof that pasteurized milk could save lives.

Emboldened by the results of these early interventions, Straus launched an extended campaign to outlaw unpasteurized milk, a battle fought ferociously by the milk industry and its representatives in statehouses around the country. Pasteurization became a political fight. Quoting an English doctor at a rally in 1907, Straus told an assembled mass of protestors: "The reckless use of raw, unpasteurized milk is little short of a national crime." Straus's advocacy attracted the attention of President Theodore Roosevelt, who ordered an investigation into the health benefits of pasteurization. Twenty government experts came to the resounding conclusion that "pasteurization prevents much sickness and saves many lives."

In 1909, Chicago became the first major American city to require pasteurization. The city's commissioner of health specifically cited the demonstrations of the "philanthropist Nathan Straus" in making the case for sterilized milk. New York followed suit in 1914. By the early 1920s, three decades after Nathan Straus opened the first milk depot on the Lower East Side, unpasteurized milk had been outlawed in almost every major American city.

Pasteurization was not the only chemistry breakthrough that transformed what people drank. Right around the time that Nathan Straus was fighting for safe milk supplies, other pioneers were introducing small amounts of chlorine into public drinking water, greatly reducing the chance of contracting diseases like cholera and typhoid.

The combination of those two interventions had a near-miraculous impact of the health of children. From 1900 to 1930, infant mortality rates in the United States dropped by 62 percent, one of the most dramatic declines in history. And that progress has continued. For every hundred human beings born in New York City for most of the nineteenth century, only sixty would make it to adulthood. Today, ninety-nine of them do.

There are still tragic gaps in the health of children between wealthy neighborhoods and low-income ones. You can travel a few stops on the 2 train in Brooklyn and find yourself in a neighborhood with twice the infant mortality rate as the one you started in. But even those low-income communities are staggeringly good at keeping babies alive compared to the 1800s. The change is so pronounced that it requires an extra decimal point. When children were drinking swill milk in the middle of the nineteenth century, childhood mortality was about 40 percent. Today, even in the worst-performing neighborhoods of New York, the infant mortality rate is 0.6 percent. The citywide average is 0.4 percent.

What were the ingredients behind such dramatic progress? Undeniably, there were the usual suspects: brilliant scientists like Louis Pasteur, supported by the technical innovations of microscopes that let humans see dangerous bacteria for the first time. But the activists like Nathan Straus were essential as well. The swill milk scandal and the fight for pasteurized milk were media events as much as they were triumphs of Enlightenment science. To make milk safe to drink, we needed a chemist using the scientific method to invent a technique that killed off the contaminants. But we also needed people willing to make some noise.

CHAPTER FIVE

BEYOND THE PLACEBO EFFECT →
(Drug Testing and Regulation)

In 1937, a Canadian graduate student named Frances Oldham wrote a letter to an accomplished chemist at the University of Chicago named Eugene Geiling asking about the possibility of a job as a research assistant in Geiling's lab. Oldham was just twenty-one years old and something of a prodigy, having graduated from high school at fifteen and having already completed a graduate degree in pharmacology. The letter so impressed Geiling that he sent a response via airmail, special delivery: "If you can be in Chicago by March 1st," he wrote, "you may have the Research Assistantship for four months and then a scholarship to see you through a PhD. Please wire immediate decision."

There was just one catch. Geiling had addressed the letter to a "Mr. Oldham." But Frances Oldham was, in fact, a woman—in an age when female biochemists were practically unheard of. "Geiling was very conservative and old-fashioned," Oldham later wrote, "and he really did not hold too much with women as scientists." She weighed sending a response back to Geiling noting the confusion. "Here my conscience tweaked me a bit," she recalled. "I knew that men were the preferred commodity in those days. Should I write and explain that Frances with an 'e' is female and with an 'i' is male?" Oldham ran the question by her university adviser, who dismissed her concerns. "Don't be ridiculous," he said. "Accept the job, sign your name, put Miss in brackets afterwards, and go!"

The decision proved to be a turning point for Oldham. "To this day," she wrote in her memoirs, "I do not know if my name had been Elizabeth or Mary Jane, whether I would have gotten that first big step up." Her timing turned out to be uncanny. Just a few months after her arrival, Geiling's lab found itself in the middle of a national life-or-death crisis—all revolving around tainted medicines.

Today we think of medicine as one of the pillars of modern progress, alongside smartphones and electric cars. Antibiotics treat many of the illnesses that killed our great-grandparents' generation; promising new immunotherapies are curing cancers; the AIDS cocktail can stop the deadly HIV virus in its tracks. But those miracle drugs are actually a remarkably recent invention. As late as the 1930s, the overwhelming majority of medicine on the market was useless, if it wasn't actively harmful. There is something puzzling about medicine's sorry state in the first half of the twentieth century. What was holding the science of medicine back, when so many other fields were climbing the ladder of progress?

There are a number of answers to that question. But one of the most important explanations is this: it simply wasn't against the law to sell junk medicine. In fact, the entire pharmaceutical industry effectively had no oversight for the first decades of the twentieth century. Technically speaking, there was an organization known as the Bureau of Chemistry, created in 1906 to oversee the industry. But the bureau had no real power to encourage the development of effective medicines. Its only responsibility was to ensure that the chemical ingredients listed on the bottle were actually present in the medicine itself. If you wanted to put mercury or cocaine in your miracle drug, the bureau had no problem with that, as long as you mentioned it on the label.

It took a national tragedy to change that preposterous state of affairs. In the early 1930s, the German drug company Bayer AG developed a new class of drug called sulfonamides, or "sulfa" drugs, one of the forerunners of modern antibiotics and one of the first medicines that actually seemed to offer some kind of benefit to the patients who used it. Within a few years, the market was flooded with copycat medicines. Unfortunately, sulfonamide was not soluble in either alcohol or water, and so the existing sulfa drugs came in the form of pills that were particularly challenging for children to swallow.

Sensing a market opportunity, a twenty-seven-year-old Tennessean named Samuel Evans Massengill dropped out of medical school to start his own drug company, with the aim of producing a sulfa variant that would be easier to consume. In 1937, the chief chemist Harold Watkins at the newly formed S. E. Massengill Company hit upon the idea of dissolving the drug in diethylene glycol, with raspberry flavoring added to make the concoction even more palatable to children. The company rushed the concoction to market under the brand Elixir Sulfanilamide, shipping 240 gallons of the medicine to pharmacies around the United States, promising a child-friendly cure for strep throat.

While sulfa was a useful medicine—and the raspberry flavoring added the "spoonful of sugar that helps the medicine go down," as Mary Poppins would say—there was a terrible flaw in Massengill's plan: diethylene glycol is toxic to humans.

Within weeks, six deaths were reported in Tulsa, Oklahoma, linked to the "elixir," each one from kidney failure. The deaths triggered a frantic nationwide search. By this point, the Bureau of Chemistry had been renamed the Food and Drug Administration (FDA), a government body that still exists today. Agents from the FDA pored over pharmacy records, alerted doctors, and warned anyone who had purchased the drug to immediately destroy it. But the FDA didn't have enough scientific expertise on staff to determine what made the drug so lethal. And so they asked a chemist at the University of Chicago named Eugene Geiling to do his own investigation. Within weeks, Geiling had his entire team of graduate students, including his new addition, Frances Oldham, testing all the ingredients of the medicine on animals in his lab. Geiling quickly identified diethylene glycol—a close chemical relative of the antifreeze used in automobiles—as the culprit.

Geiling's team had done brilliant scientific detective work. But for many families around the United States, it came too late. By the time the FDA recovered the last bottle, seventy-one adults and thirty-four children had died from consuming the elixir. Many more had been hospitalized with severe kidney problems, narrowly avoiding death.

Amazingly, at that moment in American history, the government still lacked a key leadership position that had direct oversight over the nation's health. (The Department of Health, Education, and Welfare was not created until 1953.) Management of this deadly drug crisis fell to Henry Wallace, then the secretary of agriculture. Hauled before Congress to explain how this poison had made its way into consumers' hands, Wallace explained that the FDA had, in fact, performed its official duties. "Before the elixir was put on the market, it was tested for flavor but not for its effect on human life," Secretary Wallace later reported to congress. "The existing Food and Drugs Act does not require that new drugs be tested before they are placed on sale." The examiners at the FDA had confirmed that Elixir Sulfanilamide tasted like raspberries as advertised. They just didn't bother to investigate whether it caused kidney failure.

The Elixir Sulfanilamide tragedy revealed that something important was missing in the entire system of how drugs were created and sold. No one was testing these drugs to ensure that they were safe. As long as their lists of ingredients were correct, the drug manufacturers had free rein to sell whatever miracle potion they wanted. Even when one of those ingredients happened to be a known poison that killed 104 people, the penalty was only a financial slap on the wrist.

Outraged citizens pressed for reform, and in 1938 President Franklin Roosevelt signed the Food, Drug, and Cosmetics Act into law. For the first time, the FDA was empowered to investigate the safety of all drugs sold in the United States. At long last, the regulators could look beyond the raspberry flavoring to the more pressing question of whether the drug in question might kill you.

The 1938 act was an important step forward, but it was only half of the solution that was ultimately needed. The FDA had been given authority to test drugs to confirm that they were safe. But they still had no power to ensure that the medicines actually *worked*.

You might think that consumers would ultimately punish the drugmakers selling false cures. That's the way it works in normal markets. If one company consistently sells television sets that don't work, eventually consumers catch on and stop buying that brand. But medicine is a strange exception, for two reasons. The first is the placebo effect: on average, human beings do tend to see improved health outcomes when they are told they are being given a useful medicine, even if the medicine they're taking is a sugar pill. How placebos actually work is still not entirely understood, but the effect is real. There is no equivalent placebo effect for, say, televisions or shoes. If you go into business selling fake televisions, 20 percent of customers are not going to somehow imagine fake television shows when they get their purchase back to their living rooms. But a pharmaceutical company selling fake elixirs will reliably get positive outcomes from a meaningful portion of its customers because of the placebo effect.

The other reason unregulated markets fail with medicine is that human beings have their own internal pharmacy in the form of their immune systems. Most of the time, when people get sick, they get better on their own because the immune system has the ability to recognize and fight off threats or injuries and repair damage.

Thanks to the placebo effect and the immune system, as long as the magic elixir didn't cause kidney failure, drugmakers could sell their concoction to consumers, and most of the time those consumers would indeed see results. Their strep throat would subside, or their fever would go down—not because they'd ingested some quack's miracle formula, but because their immune system was quietly, invisibly doing its job. From the patient's point of view, however, the miracle formula deserved all the credit.

Why didn't the FDA start evaluating drugs to see if they actually worked in 1938, when they started testing for safety? The answer to that question involves one of the most important revolutions in the history of human health. It wasn't a revolution that's easy to see—like vaccines or pasteurized milk. It was a revolution in statistics and what we call experiment design. The only people who really paid attention to it at the time were research scientists. But it changed life for the better. The technical term for this breakthrough idea is a mouthful: randomized controlled double-blind experiments, known as RCTs.

The reason the FDA did not test to see if the drugs worked in 1938 is that they didn't have a rigorous way of answering that question—testing for what we call the drug's *efficacy*. But just ten years later, all that started to change thanks to the pioneering work of a handful of scientists and statisticians, most famously a British epidemiologist named Austin Bradford Hill. Hill conducted the very first RCT in the late 1940s, studying the effects of antibiotics on the deadly disease tuberculosis. That study was a true milestone in the history of medicine, and it became a template for just about every study of drug efficacy since, including the experimental trials in 2020 that proved that the new mRNA vaccines could successfully combat the coronavirus.

The RCT is a surprisingly simple technique—so simple, in fact, that it begs the question of why it took so long for people to discover it. The main ingredients of an RCT are visible in the term itself: randomized, double-blind, and controlled. Say you are testing a new drug that allegedly cures strep throat. First, you find a large number of people who currently are suffering from the illness, and you randomly divide them into two groups. One group—known as the experimental group—will receive the medicine you are testing; the other will receive a placebo. The placebo group is the control, a kind of yardstick against which you can measure the effectiveness of the drug. The control group measures how long it takes for strep throat to be naturally cured by the body's immune system.

If the medicine in question actually works, the group that has received the drug will get better faster than the control group. If there's no difference in outcome between the two—or if the experimental group starts dying of kidney failure—you know you have a problem with the drug you are testing. Crucially, neither the people administering the experiment nor its participants know which subject is in which group—that's why it's called a "double-blind" experiment. Withholding that knowledge prevents subtle forms of bias from creeping into the study.

Put all those elements together, and you have a system for separating the quack cures from the real thing, or for detecting dangerous side effects in consumer or industrial products. (One of the most influential early RCTs from the 1950s made the first convincing case that smoking was causing lung cancer.) When Frances Oldham began her career investigating Elixir Sulfanilamide, she had no access to the experimental breakthrough of the RCT, which made it impossible to tell whether new drugs were actually working. But decades later, she would play a key role in another mass tragedy triggered by a new drug, one that would ultimately make RCTs an essential tool in approving new medication.

In August of 1960, Oldham—now known by her married name of Frances Oldham Kelsey—took a job at the FDA as one of only three medical reviewers assessing the applications for new drugs. The FDA's oversight of the drug industry had expanded since the days of Elixir Sulfanilamide, but manufacturers still had no obligation to submit proof that the new drug actually worked. If the FDA was satisfied that the new drug wasn't dangerous, the agency would allow the pharma companies to bring it to market. The manufacturers could stir together a random mix of ingredients and call it a cure for arthritis, and as long as it didn't contain any known toxins, they could sell it by the barrel to unwitting customers.

A few weeks after starting her new job at the FDA, an application for the production and sale of a new sleeping pill called thalidomide—marketed in the United States as Kevadon—came across her desk. (It was also prescribed as a remedy for morning sickness in newly pregnant women.) Because thalidomide had been approved for use throughout Europe, the American company that had licensed the drug submitted a brief application, assuming the drug would get a quick approval. But Kelsey insisted on doing more research and soon found evidence from the UK suggesting that there was nerve damage associated with the sleeping pill. Facing serious pushback from the manufacturer, she delayed the approval—in part because she was worried about the the risk of nerve damage on a growing fetus.

Her concern proved to be a tragically perceptive one. Unbeknownst to Kelsey, German doctors had already begun reporting an unusual surge in children born with severely malformed limbs, a condition known as phocomelia. Half of the newborns died. Once again, a frantic race to identify the culprit began. By the fall of 1961, with the Kevadon application still under review in the United States thanks to Kelsey's objections, European authorities had convincingly linked thalidomide to the wave of birth defects. In March 1962, the manufacturer formally withdrew its application.

More than ten thousand children were born around the world with phocomelia that had been caused by thalidomide, and an untold number of women lost their pregnancies. Only a handful of cases were reported in the United States. Americans had been spared the tragedy of thalidomide

thanks to the discerning eye of Frances Oldham Kelsey and her colleagues at the FDA. In a Rose Garden ceremony, President Kennedy awarded her the President's Award for Distinguished Federal Civilian Service. "I thought that I was accepting the medal on behalf of a lot of different federal workers," she later wrote in her memoirs. "This was really a team effort."

Frances Oldham Kelsey receiving her award from President Kennedy

Like the Elixir Sulfanilamide crisis before it, the thalidomide scandal immediately opened doors of new legislation that activists had been leaning against unsuccessfully for years. Within a few months of thalidomide being pulled off the market, Congress passed a new landmark law that radically extended the demands made on new drug applicants. For the first time, drug companies would be required to supply proof of efficacy, not just safety. It wasn't enough for the drug companies to offer evidence that they weren't poisoning their customers. Now, at long last, they would have to actually show proof that they were curing them.

Today, we all benefit from that historic breakthrough: when we visit the drugstore to pick up a prescription for an illness, we can have confidence that the drugs are largely safe and effective. That confidence is the result of two major innovations: the experimental breakthrough of the RCT, and the establishment of institutions like the FDA that monitor new drugs.

We do not typically hear a lot about heroic government regulators. The power of an effective bureaucracy like the FDA lies partly in the way its intelligence and expertise is distributed across thousands of people, each quietly doing their job: reviewing the clinical records, interviewing the applicants, trying to understand the problem at hand with as much rigor as possible. But we can see the benefits of government oversight in the sheer scale of the lives saved once the regulators were actually allowed to investigate the safety of the drugs being sold to the American people. Those benefits have real numbers behind them. The 104 people who lost their lives to Elixir

Sulfanilamide would have survived had the FDA done the simplest tests on the drug. And if Frances Oldham Kelsey had arrived on the job just sixty days later than she did, consider the thousands of Americans who might have been born with terrible physiological disadvantages—or who might never have been born at all.

CHAPTER SIX

THE MOLD THAT CHANGED THE WORLD
(Antibiotics)

In December 1940, a policeman named Albert Alexander decided to do some late-season gardening at his home in Oxford, England. At some point during his work, he leaned too closely into a rosebush, and a thorn from the plant scratched his face.

At first glance, it seemed to be a trivial injury, the sort of thing you patch up with a Band-Aid and forget about three days later. But Constable Alexander's wound turned out to be infected by two kinds of bacteria, with the technical names *Staphylococcus* and *Streptococcus*. (If you've ever had strep throat, you were fighting off an infection of *Streptococcus*.) Within a matter of weeks, the infection had spread throughout his body, and he was seriously ill. By February, Alexander's body was oozing pus and he had lost an eye to the infection. It was clear to his doctors that the policeman had only days left to live.

The idea of losing your life because of a gardening scratch seems all out of proportion to us today, but as late as 1940, this kind of infection was a regular occurrence. Bacterial infections not only made seemingly minor injuries potentially fatal, they also made it risky to undergo surgical procedures. Many people—particularly injured soldiers returning from the battlefield— died in hospitals not because of their initial condition or wound, but because they acquired a bacterial infection while undergoing surgery. And bacterial diseases like tuberculosis were deadly killers as well. For most of the nineteenth century, tuberculosis was responsible for as many as a quarter of all recorded deaths in the United States.

Today, all that has changed. It is almost impossible to die from a rose thorn scratch. Surgeries have become so much safer that a whole new class of "elective" procedures have become commonplace—everything from repairing minor sports injuries to plastic surgery. Tuberculosis is not even listed in the top fifty causes of death in the United States.

Albert Alexander played a crucial part in that extraordinary revolution, though he ultimately did not recover from his rose thorn infection. His claim to fame is that he was the first person to receive a medical dose of penicillin, the first antibiotic, the wonder drug that truly changed the world.

The discovery of penicillin is one of the few medical breakthroughs—alongside Edward Jenner's smallpox vaccine—that will sometimes be included in history books. But like Jenner and the milkmaids, the story of penicillin's discovery that most people have heard is too simple and neglects one of the most important elements of the achievement.

Alexander Fleming

The traditional story goes like this: On a fateful day in September 1928, the Scottish scientist Alexander Fleming accidentally left a petri dish containing the bacteria *Staphylococci* exposed to the elements next to an open window and then departed for a two-week vacation. When he returned to his lab on September 28, he discovered a blue-green mold growing in the petri dish. Before he could throw it away, Fleming noticed something strange: the mold appeared to have stopped the growth of the bacteria. Looking at the mold under a microscope, he saw that the mold was actually breaking down the cell walls of the bacteria, effectively destroying them.

It was the holy grail: a bacteria killer. Fleming called it *penicillin*. Seventeen years later, after the true magnitude of his discovery had become apparent, he was awarded the Nobel Prize in Medicine.

The Fleming story has traveled so widely in part because it has served as a justification for anyone who keeps a messy desk at work. If Fleming had been just a little tidier, he wouldn't have accidentally left out that petri dish, and he probably wouldn't have received that Nobel. But the discovery of penicillin was not just a matter of a happy accident. It also had to do with Fleming's curiosity. Fleming was the sort of person who sought out interesting developments in chaotic environments. He was an avid game player, both at work and in leisure. Whatever amusement he happened to be pursuing—golf or billiards or cards—he was constantly inventing new rules on the fly, sometimes midgame. When asked to describe his work, he would often describe it with a seemingly self-deprecating "I play with microbes." But he meant it seriously. A mind less drawn to surprising, unplanned discoveries would have taken one look at that moldy petri dish and dismissed it as garbage, a spoiled experiment. Fleming assumed it was interesting. That is often how new ideas come into the world: someone perceives a signal where others would instinctively perceive noise.

But Fleming was only part of the penicillin story, and discovering the mold was only the first step to making a world-changing medicine. Like so many stories of genuine breakthroughs, the tale of the petri dish and the open window massively compresses the real narrative of how penicillin—and the antibiotics that quickly followed in its wake—came to transform the world. The triumph of penicillin is actually one of the great stories of international, multidisciplinary collaboration. It is a story of a network, not an eccentric genius.

Fleming was a member of that network, but only one of many. He seemed to have not entirely grasped the true potential of what he had stumbled upon. He failed to set up the most basic of experimental trials to test penicillin's efficacy at killing bacteria outside the petri dish.

The real challenge with penicillin was figuring out a way to manufacture it at scale. Fleming himself never even tried to solve that problem; he moved on after making his famous discovery and did very little work attempting to address the scaling issues.

It took two other Oxford scientists, Howard Florey and Ernst Boris Chain, to turn penicillin from a curiosity to a lifesaver. Their work didn't begin for more than a decade after Fleming's original discovery. Global events had turned the mold from a potential medical breakthrough into a key military asset: World War II had broken out, and it was clear that a miracle drug that reduced the death rate from infections would be a major boost to the side who was first able to develop it.

In many ways, the race to develop penicillin was similar to the race to develop the atomic bomb, involving brilliant scientists and top-secret operations. But with penicillin, the race was not to invent a destructive weapon but rather a new way of keeping people alive.

One of the key milestones in that race involved Constable Albert Alexander. Florey and Chain had started conducting experiments with penicillin in 1939. With the help of a clever jack-of-all-trades engineer named Norman Heatley, they had built an elaborate contraption that could convert twelve liters of broth filled with the penicillin mold into two liters of penicillin medication in just an hour. It wasn't a lot of medicine by modern standards, but it was far more than their original supply.

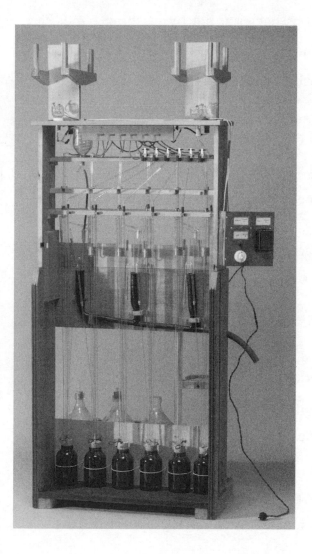

A re-creation of Norman Heatley's penicillin-producing contraption

After experimenting with mice, Florey and Chain decided they were ready to try their new treatment on an actual human. They found Alexander in a nearby hospital "desperately and pathetically ill." Within hours, Alexander began to heal. It was like watching a reverse horror movie: a man whose body had been visibly disintegrating suddenly switching directions. His temperature settled back to a normal range, and for the first time in days he could see through his remaining eye. The pus that had been dripping from his scalp entirely disappeared.

As they watched Alexander's condition improve, Florey and his colleagues recognized they were seeing something genuinely new. "Chain was dancing with excitement," a colleague would write of the momentous day. "Florey [was] reserved and quiet but nonetheless intensely thrilled by this remarkable clinical story." For the first time in our long history, humans had devised a technique to kill dangerous bacteria, not by washing hands or purifying water systems but by engineering a new compound that could be ingested by infected people and distributed through their bloodstream to attack the killer microbes.

Yet for all their genius, Florey and Chain had not yet solved the scale problem. In fact, they had such limited supplies of penicillin that they took to recycling the compound that had been excreted in Alexander's urine. After two weeks of treatment, they ran out of the medicine. Alexander's condition immediately worsened, and on March 15 the policeman died, killed by that rose thorn scratch.

Alexander's remarkable, if temporary, recovery had made it clear that penicillin could cure people of deadly bacterial infections. What was less clear was whether enough could be produced to make a difference.

To solve the scale problem, Howard Florey turned to the Americans. He wrote Warren Weaver, the visionary head of the Rockefeller Foundation, explaining the promising new medicine. Weaver recognized the significance of the finding and arranged to have the penicillin—and the Oxford team—brought over to the United States to pursue their research there, far from the

German bombs that had started raining down on England. On July 1, 1941, Florey and Heatley took a Pan Am Clipper aircraft from Lisbon, Portugal, carrying a locked briefcase containing a significant portion of the world's supply of penicillin.

In America, the team was quickly set up with a lab at the Department of Agriculture's Northern Regional Research Laboratory in Peoria, Illinois. Almost immediately the project attracted the support of the US military, who were understandably eager to find a miracle drug that would protect its troops from the infections that had killed so many soldiers in past conflicts. Before long, several American drug companies, including Merck and Pfizer, were enlisted as part of the project as well, given their expertise at mass-production.

It might seem strange that Florey and Chain were set up in an agricultural lab when they were working on a medical drug. But Peoria turned out to be the perfect spot for them. The agricultural scientists had extensive experience with molds and other soil-based organisms. And the heartland location had one meaningful advantage: its proximity to corn. Penicillin turned out to thrive in vats of corn steep liquor, which was a waste product created by making cornstarch.

While the scientists experimented with creating larger yields of penicillin in the corn steep liquors, they also suspected that there might be other strains of it out in the wild that would be easier to grow rapidly. Maybe there was some other mold lying in the dirt somewhere that could be scaled up even faster than Fleming's discovery.

And that is how the United States government came to launch one of the greatest needle-in-a-haystack operations in the history of the world, only in this case, the needle was a mold that might have been invisible to the naked eye, and the haystack was anywhere on the planet that had live soil. While Allied soldiers fought the iconic battles of World War II, dozens of soldiers quietly pursued a separate mission all around the world, a mission that, on the face of it, seemed closer to kindergarten recess than military action—literally digging in the dirt, collecting soil samples to be shipped to the American labs for investigation. One of those expeditions brought back an organism that would become the basis for streptomycin, now one of the most widely used antibiotics in the world.

They searched for promising molds closer to home as well. During the summer months of 1942, shoppers in local grocery stores in Peoria began to notice a strange presence in the fresh produce aisles: a young woman intently examining the fruit on display, picking out and purchasing the ones with visible rot. She must have seemed to be an eccentric customer to the grocers and checkout clerks, but in reality she was on a top-secret mission, integral to the life or death of millions of Allied troops fighting the war.

Her name was Mary Hunt, and she was a bacteriologist from the Peoria lab assigned the task of locating promising molds that might replace the existing strains that were being used to make penicillin. (Her unusual shopping habits ultimately gave her the nickname Moldy Mary.) One of Hunt's molds—growing in a particularly unappetizing cantaloupe—turned out to be far more productive than the original strains that Florey and Chain's team had tested. It proved to be a transformative discovery. Nearly every strain of penicillin in use today descends from the bacterial colony Hunt found in that cantaloupe.

Aided by the advanced production techniques of the drug companies, the United States was soon mass-producing a stable penicillin in quantities sufficient to be distributed to military hospitals around the world. When the Allied troops landed on France's Normandy beaches on June 6, 1944, they were carrying penicillin along with their weapons.

What was the impact of antibiotic revolution, all told? Beyond helping the United States and its allies win World War II, penicillin and the other antibiotics developed soon after the war ended triggered a revolution for human health. Mass killers like tuberculosis were almost entirely eliminated. People stopped getting severe infections from simple cuts and scrapes, like the rose thorn scratch that killed Albert Alexander. The magical power of antibiotics to ward off infection also opened the door to new treatments: radical surgical procedures like organ transplants became mainstream.

The antibiotics revolution also marked a turning point in the history of medicine. With antibiotics, the sorry track record of medical drugs finally began to change; physicians now had genuinely useful medicines to prescribe. Over the subsequent decades, antibiotics were joined by other new forms of treatment: the antiretroviral drugs that have saved so many HIV-positive people from the death sentence of AIDS, the statins and ACE inhibitors used to treat heart disease, and now a new regime of immuno-therapies that hold the promise of curing certain forms of cancer for good.

Hospitals became no longer a place people went simply to die, offering nothing but bandages and cold comfort. Now, routine surgical procedures rarely result in life-threatening infections. Quack cures remain on the market, but most of the items offered for sale by reputable drug companies actually perform as advertised. It took longer than we might have naturally expected, but today's medical healers, armed with penicillin and its many descendants, have finally developed the ability to *cure* diseases, not just prevent them.

For understandable reasons, the history of innovation—medical or otherwise—tends to be organized around momentous, singular break-throughs: penicillin or the smallpox vaccine. But it can sometimes be as instructive to investigate why a specific breakthrough *didn't* come into being in a given society. The question of why the Nazis were not able to develop an atomic bomb—and the potential consequences if they had been able to—has been pondered many times over the years. But just as interesting is the question of why they were unable to develop penicillin.

One factor was undoubtedly the secrecy that surrounded the project on the American side. While Fleming's original work, along with some of the Oxford breakthroughs, were a matter of public record, by the time the team began making significant progress in Peoria, the US government had recognized the strategic advantage that the miracle drug might give them against the Nazis. Twelve days after Pearl Harbor, President Roosevelt established an emergency wartime agency known as the Office of Censorship, assigned the task of monitoring and impeding the flow of information to America's enemies. In subsequent histories, the office's most celebrated activities involved its top-secret support of the Manhattan Project, which was the code name for the program to develop an atomic weapon. But the day after Roosevelt created the office, the team in Peoria was informed that "any information relevant to the production and use [of penicillin] should be severely restricted."

The Nazi regime did make some attempts to produce the drug at a large scale. A small team of scientists at Hoechst Dye Works began investigating the drug in 1942, but the project lagged far behind the developments in Peoria. Hoechst was not able to shift from small-batch laboratory production to factory production until late 1944. Adolf Hitler and his deputies appear to have recognized the potential benefit of the drug; a cable from Nazi headquarters in Berlin to Hoechst in March of 1945 demanded an accounting of how many tons of penicillin they could produce each day. Even at that stage, the request was delusional; the Hoescht chemical plants were nowhere near that level of productive capacity. And just days after the cable arrived, the Hoescht Dye Works was seized by Allied soldiers, putting an end to the Nazis' belated quest for the miracle drug.

There is a curious footnote to the story of penicillin and World War II. On July 20, 1944, a little more than a month after the Allied forces had landed at Normandy, a bomb planted in a conference room at the Wolf's Lair military headquarters nearly assassinated Hitler. During the blast, Hitler suffered cuts, abrasions, and burns; many of his wounds contained wooden splinters from the conference room table that had protected him from the full force of the blast—precisely the kind of wound that could lead to a deadly infection. Hitler's doctor, Theodor Morell, treated his wounds with a mysterious powder. In his journals, Morell referred to Hitler as Patient A; his notes from that night read as follows:

Patient A: eye drops administered, conjunctivitis in right eye. One fifteen P.M. Pulse 72. Eight P.M. Pulse 100, regular, strong, blood pressure 165–170. Treated injuries with penicillin powder.

Where did Morell get this penicillin? The Hoescht labs had barely begun even small-scale production in July 1944, and it was unclear whether the drugs they were producing at that stage were even effective. But Morell had access to another supply of the miracle drug, a few ampules that had been discovered on captured American soldiers and passed on to Morell by a German surgeon.

After the July 20 bombing, another doctor implored Morell to use some of the stolen antibiotics to treat another Nazi who had been horribly injured in the blast. Morell refused, presumably reserving his supply of high-grade penicillin for Hitler himself. One can only speculate on the course of events that would have followed if Hitler had developed the same sort of fatal infection that had taken Albert Alexander's life. Almost certainly the war would have ended months earlier than it did. Whatever the implications, Dr. Morell's journal entry does suggest an ironic twist to the story of the international network that brought penicillin to the masses. Fleming, Florey, Chain, Heatley, Mary Hunt—they all played an integral role in helping the Allies triumph over Nazi Germany. They also may have saved Hitler's life.

CHAPTER SEVEN

THE ROCKET SLED →
(Automobile Safety)

On August 31, 1869, the Irish scientist and aristocrat Mary Ward went for a drive with her husband and cousin through the back roads of County Offaly in the Irish midlands. They were riding in an experimental steam-powered vehicle, a predecessor of the automobile. (Her cousin's sons had built the prototype steam-car themselves.) It was typical of Ward to be toeing such adventurous waters. Despite the gender conventions of the day, she had carved a career for herself as an astronomer and a science writer; she was particularly adept at using the newly crafted microscopes that were appearing during this period, powered by those new glass lenses that were about to reveal an entire hidden ecosystem of microbes. She was also an accomplished artist. Ward published several books featuring elaborate illustrations of what she had uncovered in her own microscopic explorations.

Ward had followed a noteworthy path in the years preceding that August day in 1869; had she lived to a ripe old age and died in her sleep, she would have been remembered for her achievements as a scientist—and as a popular-izer of science—in an age where such achievements were hard fought when the scientist in question was a woman. But instead she is mostly remembered for how that admirable life ended.

The modern eye would not be impressed with the cumbersome steam-car that Ward and her fellow riders were traveling in. The technology was known as "road locomotion" in the jargon of the day. It had the centaur-like look of a miniature train attached to the back of a (horseless) carriage. Driver and pas-sengers sat up front and controlled the wheels with a lever. But as awkward as the device would look now, there was an understandable logic to it given the technology that had preceded it. Steam-powered locomotion had revolution-ized travel by rail. The next frontier was sure to be the existing road system. And so a whole generation of engineers slapped miniaturized steam engines onto drive trains and starting whirling around the countryside.

Whirling might have been an overstatement. The maximum speed of these vehicles was somewhere in the range of ten miles per hour, and most local ordinances that had managed to keep up with the technology forbade drivers to exceed five miles per hour. But the road locomotives were heavy enough to be menaces even at those low speeds. Subsequent testimony estimated that the vehicle carrying Ward was traveling less than four miles per hour on that August day in 1869. But rounding a sharp corner near a church in the town of Parsonstown, a sudden jolt threw Ward from the carriage. The rear wheels of the vehicle crushed her neck. After her husband and a fellow passenger leapt from the vehicle, they found her in convulsions and bleeding from her ears, mouth, and nose. Within minutes she was dead.

The next day the local paper ran a mournful account of her death. "The utmost gloom pervades the town," it read, "and on every hand sympathy is expressed with the husband and family of the accomplished and talented lady who has been so prematurely hurried into eternity." Short notices on the accident appeared in papers across England and Ireland, with headlines like "Fatal Accident to a Lady" and "Fearful Death of a Lady." The readers of those news items had no idea that Ward's accident would turn out to be the first in an unimaginably long list of fatalities with the same underlying culprit. The cause of death was ultimately determined by the coroner to be a broken neck, and a jury subsequently declared the death an accident. But attributing her death to a broken neck was like attributing a cholera death to dehydration. It was technically true, but the real villain was elsewhere. Ward was killed by a machine. She is believed to be the first person to die in a motor vehicle accident.

Given the existing categories utilized by mortality reports during that period, Mary Ward's death was likely included in the "accident" category.

But soon enough, public health officials had to introduce a new, more specific category into the taxonomy: automobile deaths. Just as medicine was finally maturing into a genuinely life-saving practice in the middle of the twentieth century, a new self-imposed threat emerged to shorten our lives. Back when Henry Ford was inventing the Model T, tuberculosis was the third leading cause of death in the United States. But by the time antibiotics reached the masses in the early 1950s, it had been replaced on the list by the entirely man-made menace of the automobile.

Most of the story of our doubled life expectancy comes from triumphing over natural threats that we had faced for thousands of years: killer viruses or bacterial infections. But starting in the nineteenth century a genuinely new kind of threat emerged, one that required a different set of solutions to combat. For the first time in history, large numbers of people began dying in machine-related accidents. Industrial accidents killed or injured people in the new factories that were being built. Railway and then airplane accidents began killing hundreds of people in a matter of seconds. But the deadliest invention of all was the one that killed Mary Ward.

Exactly how many human lives were sacrificed to the twentieth century's love affair with automobiles? Global numbers are difficult to estimate, but in the United States, accurate records have been kept since 1913. In a little more than a century of driving, more than four million people have died in car accidents. Three times as many Americans died in automobiles than died in all military conflicts going back to the Revolutionary War.

The impact of automobile deaths on life expectancy was particularly intense because so many of the deaths involved young people. One way to register how extensive that death toll was is to note how many celebrities died before the age of fifty in car accidents: the musicians Harry Chapin, Marc Bolan, and Eddy Cochran; the dancer Isadora Duncan; the writers Margaret Mitchell, Albert Camus, and Nathaniel West. Members of royal families died tragically young in widely covered accidents, most famously Astrid of Sweden and England's Diana, Princess of Wales. The fathers of Bill Clinton and Barack Obama both died in automobile accidents at an early age. Car crashes took the lives of the actors Jane Mansfield and Paul Walker. But few automobile deaths resonated with the general public as widely as the 1955 death of movie star James Dean, at the age of twenty-four, who was killed when his Porsche Spyder collided with a Ford Tudor at an intersection in central California.

At the time of Dean's death, almost every car manufactured offered minimal safety features. Seat belts were practically nonexistent and rarely worn; recessed steering wheels and crumple zones were unheard of; airbags and anti-lock brake systems hadn't been invented yet. The Chevrolet Bel Air, 1955's bestselling family car, had no headrests, no rearview mirrors, no padding on the dashboard, and no seat belts.

The problem with automobile safety was not so much the result of technological limitations but rather the result of faulty assumptions. People just assumed it was impossible to make cars safe. If you were going to travel at sixty miles per hour in a small metal box, there was no way to prevent loss of life if you happened to crash into another person traveling at a comparable speed. The forces in a crash were too great, and the human body was too fragile.

Making cars less deadly ultimately required a great deal of technical ingenuity. But the first step was getting people just to change their minds about the *possibility* of safer cars.

Perhaps the most important early figure to embrace that belief was a Brooklyn-born pilot and engineer who managed to get a revolutionary perspective on the problem of car safety through an experience that almost took his own life: by dropping out of the sky in an airplane.

One day in 1917, Hugh DeHaven, then a twenty-two-year-old student pilot, took off on an aerial gunnery training session in Texas overseen by the Canadian Royal Flying Corps, where DeHaven was a cadet. Something in the session went horribly awry, and DeHaven's plane collided with another aircraft participating in the training. DeHaven suffered severe internal injuries; everyone else involved in the crash perished.

In the months of recovery that followed, DeHaven found himself dwelling on the different outcomes of the crash. Why had he been spared? DeHaven had a radical idea: something in the design of the plane had protected him.

Years later, he picked up this early hunch and began investigating how what he called the "packaging" of a vehicle could protect the human body, even in high-speed collisions.

DeHaven started with eggs. He transformed his kitchen into a crash impact laboratory, with layers of foam rubber lining the floor. He would drop eggs from ten feet high on varying levels of foam, recording which materials kept the eggs from breaking on impact. Eventually, when the ceiling height of his kitchen began restricting his work, he started dropping eggs from the tops of buildings in experimental packages designed to reduce the force of the impact on the ground. (Many science classes today feature egg-drop competitions based on DeHaven's original research.) By the 1940s he could drop an egg from the top of a ten-story building without damaging the shell.

He also investigated cases where people had survived falls from great heights, collecting newspaper clippings and analyzing the forces on the human body from impact. Eventually he published his findings in an important paper in 1942, arguing that high impact collisions were not necessarily death sentences if the body was protected in specific ways.

DeHaven had made his argument with eggs and physics equations and newspaper clippings. But sometimes a different kind of persuasion is required to change the conventional wisdom. In the story of auto safety, that mode of persuasion is best exemplified by Colonel John Stapp. Stapp was a classic polymath: a surgeon, biophysicist, and pilot. He was known for a time as the fastest man on earth. The nickname was somewhat ironic, because his real legacy was all about what happens to the human body when it slows down.

In the 1950s, building on DeHaven's research, Stapp was researching plane crashes at the Aero Medical Lab. He had developed a new kind of technology that would perform stress analysis on actual human bodies—as well as what became known as crash-test dummies. The technical term for the device they invented was the "linear decelerator." But it became known by a more catchy name: the rocket sled.

Rocket sleds were effectively a pack of solid rocket-fuel motors strung on the back of a sled carrying a single passenger, usually sitting upright strapped into a padded chair. The whole contraption slid over precisely aligned rails to keep it from veering off in random directions. (There were no wheels involved.) The brake systems were robust enough that they

The original "Sonic Wind" linear decelerator

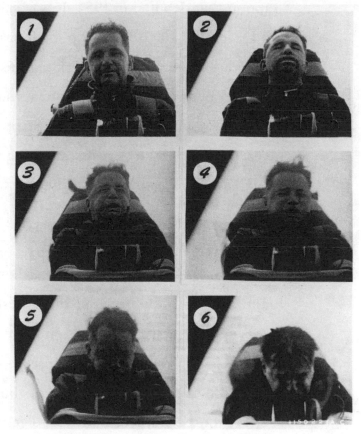

Colonel John Stapp during the final seconds of his December 1954 ride

could bring a sled traveling at 120 miles per hour to a standstill in just a few seconds. Early versions could hit top speeds in the 200s.

Stapp was not just a designer; he was an active user of the device. Over the years he broke ribs, fractured his wrist twice, and suffered temporary vision loss. But each time he rode the device, a small battalion of sensors were dutifully taking notes on the slightest changes in his body as it battled those prodigious forces.

John Stapp is now mostly remembered for his involvement with a contraption that debuted in 1954. It was called the Sonic Wind Rocket Sled 1. On December 10, 1954, Stapp made history on the Holloman High Speed Test Track in New Mexico by riding the Sonic Wind at a peak speed of 628 miles per hour before slamming to a death-defying halt in just 1.4 seconds.

Think about how courageous Stapp had to be to conduct this experiment. It was not at all clear that traveling over land at near the speed of sound was a survivable experience. While he was strapped into a throne-like seat with carefully positioned restraints, he performed the test without any kind of protection over his face.

No human being had ever traveled on land at anywhere near that speed. Stapp was instantly declared the fastest man on earth, appearing on the cover of *Life* magazine—the pinnacle of American media during that period—in early 1955. It wasn't pretty—Stapp again lost vision temporarily, and his face was badly bruised—but he was alive at the end of it and suffered no permanent injuries. "I felt a sensation in the eyes," he later recalled, "somewhat like the extraction of a molar without anesthetic." But he had survived.

Stapp realized that his experiments with the rocket sled had massive implications for automobile safety. If you could decelerate from six hundred miles per hour to zero in a matter of seconds without major injuries, surely you should be able to survive a collision at sixty miles per hour. In his years in the air force, Stapp had noticed that more of his fellow servicemen died in automobiles than in airplanes. And so in May of 1955, he invited twenty-six people involved in the automobile industry to visit Holloman Air Base to witness the rocket sled in action and discuss ways in which the lessons of Stapp's research could be applied to auto safety. The sessions were repeated the next year; more than sixty years later, the Stapp Car Crash Conference is still the main industry meeting for the extended community of auto safety experts.

But even with the critical evidence that DeHaven and Stapp had compiled, the American auto industry in Detroit largely ignored the call for safety improvements. The first major breakthrough that originated with an actual car company came from Sweden. In the mid-1950s, Volvo hired an aeronautical engineer named Nils Bohlin who had been working on emergency ejection seats at Saab's aerospace division. Bohlin began tinkering with a piece of equipment that had been largely an oversight in most automobiles up until that point: the seat belt. Many cars were sold without any seat belts at all; the models that did include them offered poorly designed lap belts that provided minimal protection in the event of a crash. They were rarely worn, even by children.

Borrowing from the approach to safety restraint used by military pilots, Bohlin quickly developed what he called a three-point design. Bohlin's design brought together a shoulder and lap belt that buckled together in a V formation at the passenger's side, which meant the buckle itself wouldn't cause injuries in a collision. It was an elegant design, the basis for the seat belts that now come standard on every car manufactured anywhere in the world.

By 1959, Volvo was selling cars with the three-point seat belt as a standard feature. Early data suggested that this one addition was single-handedly reducing auto fatalities by 75 percent. Three years later, Bohlin was granted patent number 3043625 by the United States Patent Office for "three-point seat belt systems comprising two side lower and one side upper anchoring devices." Recognizing the wider humanitarian benefits of the technology, Volvo chose not to enforce the patent, making Bohlin's design freely available to all car manufacturers worldwide. The ultimate impact of Bohlin's design was staggering. More than one million lives—many of them young ones—have been saved by the three-point seat belt. A few decades after it was awarded, the Bohlin patent was recognized as one of the eight patents to have had "the greatest significance for humanity" over the preceding century.

The seat belt, of course, was just one of a series of safety innovations have transformed automobile safety. Activists compelled Congress to pass laws requiring seat belts and lowering speed limits in the 1960s. The airbag, originally invented in the 1950s, was refined by a number of engineers until becoming mandatory in 1989. Anti-lock brakes, pioneered by the airline industry, became standard in cars in the 1990s. The tragic death of her daughter in a drunk driving accident compelled Candice Lightner to form Mothers Against Drunk Driving in 1980, leading to a radical decrease in alcohol-related accidents.

What was the total impact of all these inventions and interventions? If you sit behind the wheel of an automobile today, you are more than ten times less likely to die than you would have been when automobiles first became part of modern life. Recall that car accidents were the third most common cause of death when James Dean stepped into that Porsche Spyder in 1955. Today, they are not even in the top ten.

Take a look at this chart that shows the decline in automobile fatalities in the United States from 1955 today:

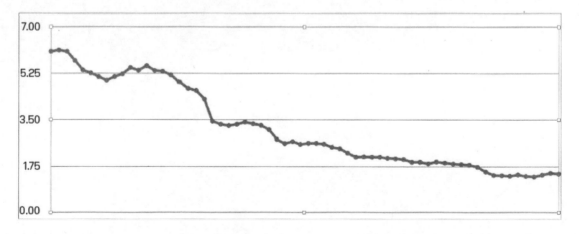

US automobile fatalities per 100 million miles driven

The most pronounced drop comes in the five years after the passage of the new laws in the 1960s, requiring seat belts and reducing top speed limits to fifty-five miles per hour. But the most striking thing about the chart is the steady, incremental improvements in safety that occurred in the following three decades. There are no sudden, dramatic improvements. Each year, with a few exceptions, is just slightly safer than the year before. That's the kind of chart you see when progress comes not from one genius inventor or dramatic breakthrough but the work of thousands, each attacking the problem from different angles: consumer advocates, industry engineers, government regulators, grief-stricken mothers.

Because each year is just a fraction better than the one before, we never hear about the improvement. Celebrity deaths and other tragic accidents continue to make headlines, but the lives saved never make it to the front page, because year by year, the changes are small. But when you stack them up over a half century of driving, they're miraculous.

CHAPTER EIGHT

FEED THE WORLD
(The Decline of Famine)

The extension of human life expectancy didn't just give us extra years of being alive. It also gave us more people. Take a look at this chart of global population, dating back to the dawn of civilization:

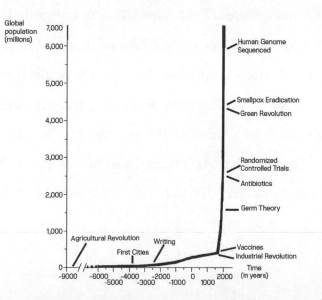

The change in the past century is shocking. We've gone from two billion humans on the planet to almost eight billion. That runaway growth in population is not the result of people having more babies. In fact, on average, people all around the world are having fewer babies per capita than ever before. What changed over the past two centuries, first in the industrialized world, then globally, is that people stopped dying—particularly young people. And by not dying most of them lived long enough to have their own children, who repeated the cycle with their children. Repeat that pattern all over the world for six or seven generations, and global population can grow from two billion to eight billion very quickly.

If you'd told someone in 1920 that global population was going to quadruple in the coming century, they would have likely reacted to the news with one major concern: How are we going to feed all those people? They would have been right to be so worried. Famines had been a major factor in reducing our lifespan since the invention of agriculture. The famous Irish potato famine of the late 1840s killed roughly one-eighth of the population and forced another quarter of the population to emigrate in search of food to other regions of the world, mostly the United States. The beginnings of what we now call the "Little Ice Age" in the 1300s brought floods and unusually cold weather to Northern Europe, producing famines that may have taken the lives of as much as a third of the population. Scholars now believe the mysterious collapse of the Mayan civilization was partially triggered by an extreme drought between 1020 and 1100 CE that led to massive crop failure, ultimately causing that advanced culture to vanish practically overnight.

A hundred years ago, the world had just experienced the Great Persian Famine of 1916–1918, where, according to some historians, as much as 50 percent of the population of modern-day Iran perished. Terrible famines were still raging in India and the newly formed Soviet Union at that time. Upwards of fifty million people died during the famines of the 1920s. Globally, starvation would continue driving down human life expectancy significantly until the 1970s.

And then, almost overnight, everything changed. Somewhere around five million people have died from famines between 1980 and today, compared to roughly fifty million over the preceding forty years. The drop is even more pronounced when you factor in global population growth during that period. Calculated on a per capita basis, famine deaths have declined from 82 per 100,000 people in the wake of the Great Persian Famine to just 0.5 per 100,000 people over the last five years.

Small-scale famines still happen, and there is every reason to believe that the deep-seated disturbances of climate change—both in terms of altered ecosystems and the demographic chaos of mass migration—will cause them to increase in the coming decades. But for the last forty years at least, the trend lines are about as encouraging as they can be.

How did we manage to feed the world despite the massive increase in population over that period? Part of the explanation lies in the invention of artificial fertilizer, a breakthrough that arrived right as the famines of the early 1920s were devastating so many nations around the world. Artificial fertilizer has a strange history. It relies on a compound known as ammonium nitrate, which had been employed by plants all around the world as a natural fertilizer to support their growth for eons. But a new use for the material opened up about a thousand years ago, when the Chinese first began experimenting with the explosive power of a close chemical relative, potassium nitrate. Also known as saltpeter, it is the primary ingredient of gunpowder.

Nitrogen itself was first isolated and named in the 1770s, during a period of rapid advances in chemistry. By the nineteenth century, it had become clear that the nitrates could be used in two very different ways: to encourage plant growth and to blow things up. But no one knew how to manufacture those nitrates. The only available option for humans who wished to use them—at war or in their gardens—was to locate natural reserves of the chemical. And that is how seagull and bat excrement became one of the most highly prized commodities of the nineteenth century.

For more than a thousand years, the indigenous populations of coastal Peru made regular voyages to scrape guano off the rocky terrain of nearby islands. Guano is basically seagull poop, and it happens to be rich in nitrates. The Peruvians used the seagull waste to turn what had been infertile desert into a thriving soil. The Inca empire shipped guano throughout South America to improve crop yields. In the early nineteenth century, Europeans finally recognized the commercial value of guano, after centuries spent paying more attention to the gold and silver of South America than its reserves of bat and seagull excrement. In 1840, Peruvians exploring the Chincha Islands off the country's southern Pacific coast made an amazing discovery: deposits of guano caked into mounds over 150 feet high, the single largest reserve of nitrates yet discovered.

At this point, the world went wild for seagull poop. Whole regions were colonized; natural ecosystems disturbed; wars were fought. Farmers all around the world used Peruvian guano to increase the fertility of the soil. Bat guano from caves in the United States was a primary resource for gunpowder for the Confederate army during the American Civil War.

The guano boom had an inevitable bust in its future, because the bats and birds simply weren't producing enough waste to keep up with the demand. In the years preceding the outbreak of World War I, Germany became increasingly concerned about its ability to generate enough bombs to fight its European rivals. The limiting factor: dwindling supplies of nitrates, originally sourced from guano. The German chemist Fritz Haber began investigating ways to synthesize nitrates in the lab, and by 1908 he had perfected a system that could create ammonium nitrate without relying on seagulls.

The industrialist Carl Bosch then designed a system where Haber's process could be reproduced at scale, with factories producing tons of ammonium nitrate. It is unclear how many deaths during the Great War might have been avoided had Haber and Bosch not teamed up to discover and amplify the technique of artificially "fixing" nitrogen. But it likely numbered in the hundreds of thousands, if not more.

Still, there was that strange property of nitrogen: it was as useful for the farmers as it was for the bomb-makers. Once you could produce nitrates in a factory, the world of agriculture lost its dependence on naturally fertile soils and bat guano. Any field, however lifeless, could be supplemented by nitrates to jump-start the soil ecosystem. Figuring out how to make more bombs turned out to help us invent an entirely new concept: artificial fertilizer.

It was a small conceptual leap, but measured in terms of twentieth century consequences, it may well be unrivaled. No single discovery had as much impact on the explosion of population growth as Haber's artificial ammonia. Artificial fertilizer—along with subsequent innovations known as the Green Revolution—made soil far more productive. Farmers could grow more crops on the same amount of land. Farmland covers about 15 percent of the earth's surface today. Without the innovations of artificial fertilizer, more than half of the ice-free land on our planet would have to be covered by farms to support a population of nearly eight billion people.

The other key innovation that helped us feed the world is a controversial one, and it's a reminder that almost every major leap forward comes with some kind of cost. Strangely enough, the story of this world-changing breakthrough begins with simple typo and an accidental entrepreneur.

In the early 1920s in Sussex County, Delaware, a young woman named Cecile Steele had been maintaining a small flock of laying chickens on her family farm, mostly to supply eggs for her family, though she would occasionally sell surplus eggs to bring in extra income. Each spring, she would order fifty additional chicks from a local hatchery. But in the spring of 1923, a mistake at the hatchery added an extra zero to her order; to Steele's surprise, five hundred chicks showed up on her doorstep.

A less enterprising customer would have simply returned the excess supply, but something about the sight of all those chicks planted an idea in Steele's mind. She stored them in an empty piano box until a lumberman could build a new shed large enough to house them. Steele fattened them up with newly invented feed supplements, and when they reached two pounds, she sold 387 of them for sixty-two cents a pound, making a tidy profit. The next year she deliberately increased the order to one thousand chickens and began scaling up the facilities on the farm.

Cecile Steele's Delaware farm

It seems strange to imagine this now—in an era where chicken has become a staple of diets all around the world, amplified by its prominence on American fast-food menus—but until the first decades of the twentieth century, chickens were largely bred for egg production, not for meat. Many households maintained their own coops and only served chicken at the dinner table when one of the birds was culled because it wasn't producing enough eggs. When Steele started her new business, most chicken purchased by restaurants or grocery store chains had been older hens, sold to be used in stews. Steele's poultry was young, which meant the meat was more tender and better suited for frying.

Five years after the fateful delivery of those five hundred chicks, Steele had built out one of the first factory-style chicken farms, raising and selling 26,000 birds in a single year. Within a few years, the number had grown to 250,000. Hundreds of farmers in the region took notice of Steele's success and launched poultry farms that emulated hers. They discovered that chicken "broilers," as they were called, were more efficient producers of protein than cattle or pigs; they required far less space and they grew to market size in just a matter of weeks, while cattle could take more than a year.

By the 1950s, the poultry industry had discovered that feeding chickens vitamin D supplements fortified with antibiotics allowed them to live indoors without exposure to sunlight; before long, industrial-scale coops crowded as many as thirty thousand chickens into wire cages so small that the birds did not have room to spread their wings.

The result was a dramatic increase in the efficiency of meat production: you could produce one pound of chicken meat with just two pounds of grain, while a pound of beef required seven pounds of grain. That led to a revolution the American diet. Fast-food chains like Kentucky Fried Chicken proliferated; McDonald's added Chicken McNuggets to its worldwide menu in 1983. Today the average American eats more than ninety pounds of chicken a year.

The change has been global as well. In 1970, Brazil produced 217 metric tons of chicken broiler meat; today they produce around 13,000 metric tons. Both China and India have seen their chicken meat production grow by more than a factor of ten over the past two decades.

But the scale of this transformation is perhaps best measured by one single datapoint: the overall population of chickens worldwide. The most numerous wild bird on the planet is the African red-billed quelea, with an estimated population of 1.5 billion. At any given moment, something in the range of *twenty-three billion* chickens are alive, and human beings consume more than sixty billion chickens each year. (The second number is so much larger because chickens are slaughtered for meat after only a few months of life.) There are now more chickens on earth than all other species of birds combined.

The rate of population growth of chickens far exceeds that of humans over the past century. But of course the two growth rates are fundamentally linked: we can support almost eight billion people on the planet now in part because we have sixty billion chickens to eat each year.

The chicken population on earth is so immense, in fact, that scholars now believe that when future archeologists thousands of years from now dig through the ruins of this era, they will use the remains of all that poultry as a key marker for the period. No doubt they will encounter other evidence of human culture: unbiodegradable plastics, buried cities, the occasional human skeleton. But the defining biological signature of the period, mummified in landfills all around the world, will be chicken bones.

The impact of the agricultural revolutions of the twentieth century—both the increase in soil fertility and the factory farming techniques that brought all those chickens into the world—stagger the mind. Experts believe that these agricultural revolutions doubled the carrying capacity of the planet, which means without these breakthroughs, half of the nearly eight billion people alive today would never have been born or would have died of starvation long ago. Countless others would have lived but at the very edge of starvation.

Lifting people out of the threat of starvation has important economic effects as well. More food on the table provides more energy for work, which ultimately pushes living standards higher. It is no accident that the nations of the world with the most spectacular rates of growth since World War II—many of them in Asia—are places where average diets have gone from borderline starvation to levels comparable to modern Europeans.

The escape from hunger is one of the great triumphs of the twentieth century, but it was not without its costs. The production of artificial fertilizers consumes as much as 5 percent of the world's natural gas supplies; artificial fertilizer runoff from farmland has created massive dead zones in seawater near river deltas, with the nitrates depriving marine life of sufficient oxygen to survive. Currently an area of more than eight thousand square miles in the Gulf of Mexico is believed to be entirely devoid of life, one of the largest dead zones ever recorded.

Many people believe that the factory farming model is also fundamentally inhumane to the animals subjected to it. These are, after all, creatures who evolved in a very different environment, being forced to live short lives in brutal conditions, all so human beings can enjoy their fast-food meals. A planet carrying twenty-three billion chickens is also running a massive and unprecedented experiment in inadvertently breeding new strains of avian flu. The H1N5 virus that provoked a global panic in 2007 was partially transmitted by chickens. If another pandemic emerges in the coming years with even more devastating effects than COVID-19's, the immense population of chickens on earth—and the systems of factory farming that produce them—is likely to be a point of origin for the outbreak.

And even if the nearly eight billion people alive today do not end up contracting new diseases, their existence puts additional strains on the planet, both in terms of environmental destruction and the output of greenhouse gases. We face the global crisis of climate change not just because we adopted an industrial lifestyle but also because we figured out new techniques to keep people from perishing in mass famines or living at the very edge of starvation.

Some of those techniques happened to have some unlikely origins—like that accidental order of chicks—but their ultimate impact is almost beyond comprehension: billions of lives lifted out of hunger and starvation, and a planet struggling to manage the secondary effects of that runaway growth.

CONCLUSION
The Work Left to Do

In May 1806, in the first few months of the second term of his presidency, Thomas Jefferson wrote a letter to Edward Jenner, the inventor of the smallpox vaccine. Jefferson had been an early adopter of vaccines, and he was writing to Jenner to express his appreciation for the doctor's lifesaving innovation. "Medicine has never before produced any single improvement of such utility," he wrote. "You have erased from the Calendar of human afflictions one of its greatest . . . Future nations will know by history only that the loathsome smallpox has existed."

Jefferson was thinking long-term about the consequences of Jenner's vaccine. In 1806, no one seriously thought that this ancient killer could be eliminated altogether. Vaccines had helped us reduce the death rate from smallpox, the first meaningful advance in extending life in our history. But entirely ridding the world of a microscopic virus? That was almost unimaginable.

A century and a half after Jefferson wrote his letter to Jenner, at the height of the Cold War, a Russian scientist addressed a gathering of the World Health Organization (WHO) and urged them to realize Jefferson's vision of smallpox eradication, quoting the American president in his speech. It was a daring, provocative challenge. Most health authorities at the time thought it was still a pipe dream. But it was the beginning of what would become one of the most inspiring and momentous achievements in the history of our species.

In 1965, an official at the Centers for Disease Control and Prevention (CDC) named D. A. Henderson wrote a proposal suggesting an approach to eliminating smallpox in West Africa. The proposal caught the eye of the White House, and in 1965 Henderson was asked to move to Geneva, Switzerland, to oversee a more ambitious program of global eradication for the WHO. Even Henderson himself thought the program would likely end in failure. But he ultimately took the assignment and oversaw a program of staggering scale and complexity.

During the decade of active surveillance and vaccination, the WHO worked in concert with seventy-three different nations and employed hundreds of thousands of health workers who oversaw vaccinations in the more than two dozen countries still suffering from smallpox outbreaks.

They were assisted by a few crucial breakthroughs that were not around when Thomas Jefferson started dreaming of smallpox eradication. The first was a scientific understanding about the virus itself. Virologists had come to believe that the smallpox virus could only survive and replicate inside human beings. Many viruses that cause disease in humans can also infect animals—think of Jenner's cowpox. But smallpox had lost the ability to survive outside of human bodies; even our close relatives among the primates are immune. This knowledge gave the eradicators a critical advantage over the virus. A traditional infectious agent under attack by a mass vaccination effort could take shelter in another host species—rodents, say, or birds. But because smallpox had abandoned whatever original host had brought it to humans, the virus was uniquely vulnerable to Henderson's campaign. If you could drive the virus out of the human population, you could truly wipe it off the face of the earth.

Technical innovations also played a crucial role in the eradication project. The invention of the bifurcated needle allowed the WHO field workers to use a multiple-puncture vaccination technique. It was both much easier to perform and required a quarter of the amount of vaccine as earlier techniques, essential attributes for an organization attempting to vaccinate millions of people around the world. Another crucial asset was a heat-stable vaccine, developed in the 1950s, that could be stored for thirty days unrefrigerated, an enormous advantage in distributing vaccines to small villages that often lacked refrigeration and electricity.

The last innovation revolved around the method of vaccinating people geographically. In December 1966, a CDC official named William Foege found himself battling an outbreak in the Liberian village of Ovirpua in West Africa. The typical response to such an outbreak would be to vaccinate every single member of the village (as well as people in nearby villages). But the CDC program was new, and sufficient supplies of vaccine had not yet been delivered. Given the limited resources, Foege was forced to improvise a solution that could do more with less.

As he later described it in his memoirs, Foege and his colleagues asked themselves the question: "If we were smallpox viruses bent on immortality, what would we do to extend our family tree? The answer, of course, was to find the nearest susceptible person in which to continue reproduction. Our task, then, was not to vaccinate everyone within a certain range but rather to identify and protect the nearest susceptible people before the virus could reach them." Instead of dumping a massive amount of vaccines on an entire region, Foege decide to create what he called a "ring" of vaccinations that would surround the infected villagers. It was a targeted strike, designed to build a firewall of immunity around the outbreak.

To Foege's surprise, it worked. Within a matter of days, the outbreak had ended. Foege's ring vaccination technique ultimately became the basis of the WHO global eradication project.

After thousands of years of conflict and cohabitation with humans, the naturally occurring smallpox virus infected its last human being in October 1975, when the telltale pustules erupted on the skin of a three-year-old Bangladeshi girl named Rahima Banu Begum.

Rahima Banu Begum and her mother

Begum lived on Bhola Island on the southern coast of Bangladesh at the mouth of the Meghna River. WHO officials were notified of the case and sent a team to treat the young girl and vaccinate all the individuals on the island who had come into contact with her. She survived her encounter with the disease, and the ring vaccinations on Bhola Island kept the virus from replicating in another host.

Four years later, after an extensive global search for other outbreaks, a commission of scientists signed a document on December 9, 1979, proclaiming that smallpox had been eradicated. In May of the following year, the World Health Assembly officially endorsed the WHO findings. Their proclamation declared that "the world and all its peoples have won freedom from small-pox," and paid tribute to the "collective action of all nations [that] have freed mankind of this ancient scourge."

It was a truly epic achievement, one that required a mix of visionary thinking and on-the-ground fieldwork spanning dozens of different countries. December 9, 1979, should be commemorated with the same measure of respect that we pay to the moon landing: a milestone in the story of human progress.

It was fitting that the most impressive feat in the history of health revolved around smallpox, since the very first breakthroughs that made a material difference in extending our lives—variolation and vaccination—were also attempts to lessen the threat of that terrible disease.

But the eradication of smallpox was just the most amazing intervention on a long list of breakthroughs that helped double life expectancy over the past century or so. This book began with two charts showing the extraordinary extension of average lifespan and the dramatic drop in childhood mortality. Those improvements happened first in industrialized countries like the United Kingdom and the United States, but thanks to more recent developments, like smallpox eradication and famine reduction, the story of increased life expectancy is now truly a global one. You can see this most clearly in this chart:

The gap between what we now generally describe as the West and the Global South has been narrowing for the past thirty years, at a rate unheard

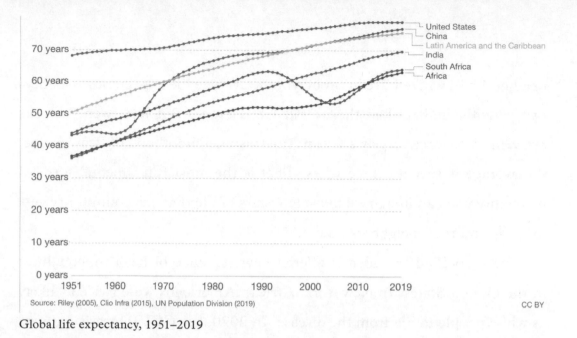

Source: Riley (2005), Clio Infra (2015), UN Population Division (2019)

Global life expectancy, 1951–2019

of in our history. It took Sweden 150 years to reduce childhood mortality rates from 30 percent to less than 1 percent. Post–World War II South Korea pulled off the same feat in just forty-six years. At the end of World War II, life expectancies in India were still trapped at just thirty-five. Today they are above seventy. In 1951, the life expectancy gap that separated China and the United States was more than twenty years. Today it is only four.

Many residents in Western countries think of the past few decades as an age of skyrocketing inequality. And, indeed, within those countries, particularly the United States, the economic outcomes in particular have been winner-take-all affairs. But when you look at the global picture of both health outcomes and income, the image inverts: it is an age of increasing equality. The lifespan gap between the richest countries and the poorest is narrowing.

As wonderful as those trendlines are, they should not be an excuse for simply sitting back and letting the march of progress continue. In the neighborhood where I live in Brooklyn, the average life expectancy is eighty-two, slightly higher than the overall US average. But just twenty blocks away, in the poorer, largely African American neighborhood of Brownsville, the average is seventy-three years. That is the most fundamental form of inequality you can imagine: almost ten years of life that one community gets to enjoy and their neighbors do not.

The COVID-19 pandemic offered new evidence of health inequalities in the United States. In New York, African Americans were twice as likely as white people to die from the disease. In 2020, the COVID crisis reduced average life expectancy in the United States by about a year. But African American men lost almost three years of life expectancy on average. Dr. Martin Luther King Jr. observed in a speech in 1966, "Of all the forms of inequality, injustice in health is the most shocking and the most inhuman." More than a half century later, we are still fighting that injustice.

COVID-19 has also reminded us that the overall trends in life expectancy are not destined to continue to rise. In the United States, for the first time since the end of the Spanish Flu, average life expectancy has decreased for four straight years, with the biggest drop in generations happening in 2020. As global temperatures rise and overall population continues to grow, it is entirely possible that the trends in aging could reverse over the next century if we don't continue the fight for healthier lives that Mary Montagu, Edward Jenner, John Snow, W. E. B. Du Bois—and all the other quiet heroes in this book—devoted their lives to.

All of which means that when we think about progress—in health or any other measure—the crucial task is to look at the data from two angles simultaneously. We need to look at past successes, both as a source of inspiration and as a template for future action. But we also need to keep an eye on all the ways in which the present is underperforming, given its potential.

What technology or intervention currently within our grasp could continue the extraordinary trends in improving human health? It's not enough simply to remind ourselves that progress is possible. It's just as important to figure out what's left to do.

ACKNOWLEDGMENTS

I suppose it would be appropriate for any book about the miracle of being alive to be dedicated to the author's mother, but in this specific case, the debt of gratitude has extra significance. For almost half a century my mother has been an inspirational agent of change in creating more equitable, more humane health-care experiences and outcomes for patients around the world. Thanks to her, I was raised to appreciate from an early age the vital role that health-care professionals play in society, and to recognize that positive change in the world of health was not just the result of scientific or technical advances but also the result of activism and advocacy, often by patients and their families themselves.

More than any of my projects, this book has benefited from an immense number of conversations with experts from the many disciplines and historical periods that it covers: Bruce Gellin, David Ho, Nancy Howell, Lorna E. Thorpe, Tara C. Smith, Marc N. Gourevitch, Linda Villarosa, Carl Zimmer, John Brownstein, Jim Kim, Samuel Scarpino, Jeremy Farrar, Andy

Slavitt, Nancy Bristow, Anthony Fauci, Clive Thompson, Joon Yun, and my multitalented cohost of the television series, David Olusoga. Max Roser and the team at Our World in Data provided invaluable help on all the vital statistics in this book. Special thanks to my brother-in-law Manesh Patel for his expert advice—and to both my parents, for so much invaluable support in such a difficult year.

A multiplatform project like this one depends on the contributions of so many different people and organizations, starting with the publishing team at Viking, including Cassie Gutman, Abigail Powers, Monique Sterling, and especially Ken Wright, who has now helped me adapt two books for younger readers. Special thanks as well to Catherine Frank for a superb edit of this version. And of course thanks to the team that published the adult version at Riverhead: my brilliant editor, Courtney Young, who managed to shepherd this book through a pregnancy and a pandemic; and my publisher, Geoffrey Kloske, who supported the project through all its many iterations.

Thanks as well to my producing partner, Jane Root, for believing in the potential of this project as a television series, and keeping the faith through a hundred near-death experiences on the way to getting it made. I'm also grateful for the stellar team that Jane has put together at Nutopia, who were instrumental both in developing the ideas in the book and the series, and in tackling the enormous logistical challenge of making a television show in the age of COVID: Fiona Caldwell, Nicola Moody, Simon Willgoss, Carl Griffin, Helena Tait, Tristan Quinn, Duncan Singh, Helen Sage, David

Alvarado, Jason Sussberg, and Jen Beamish.

I'm indebted to my longtime editor, Bill Wasik, and Jake Silverstein at the *New York Times Magazine* for seeing the potential of this project at a critical early stage. At PBS, Bill Gardner has been a tireless champion for getting these kinds of ideas on the screen since we worked together on *How We Got to Now.* I'm grateful for the financial and editorial support from the foundations and individuals who helped us make the television series, especially Doron Weber at the Sloan Foundation, and the team at the Pulitzer Center who have done such a brilliant job assembling educational materials to support this project. My agents—Lydia Wills, Ryan McNeily, Sylvie Rabineau, Travis Dunlap, and Jay Mandel—took all the various swerves of this project in stride and somehow managed to steer it to a terrific destination in the end.

Finally, thanks to my wife and sons, who truly make all this wonderful extra life worth living.

February 2022

Marin County, California

RECOMMENDED READING

For more information on the long-term trends in human health, see Steven Pinker's *Enlightenment Now*, Robert Fogel's *The Escape from Hunger and Premature Death*, and Angus Deaton's *The Great Escape*. Jennifer Carrell's *The Speckled Monster* gives an in-depth account of Mary Montagu's life and her battle to bring variolation to England. A good overview of our long struggle with the smallpox virus is Donald Hopkins's book, *The Greatest Killer*. My book *The Ghost Map* offers more information on John Snow and the waterborne theory of cholera. David Lewis's *W. E. B. Du Bois: A Biography* provides an in-depth account of Du Bois's investigation of the Seventh Ward, along with his many other achievements. The article by Tyler Moss, "The 19th-Century Swill Milk Scandal That Poisoned Infants with Whiskey Runoff," gives an excellent impression of just how unsanitary milk production was in the nineteenth century, while Mark Kurlansky's *Milk!* tells the ten-thousand-year history of the beverage. For those interested in the sorry state of medical drugs in the early twentieth century, William Rosen's *Miracle Cure* has some horrifying case studies in pharmaceutical malpractice, alongside a superb history of the invention of antibiotics. Eric Lax's *The Mold in Dr. Florey's Coat* is also a very entertaining history of penicillin. For more on the daredevils who proved that cars could be made safe, see Craig Ryan's *Sonic Wind*. G. T. Cushman's *Guano and the Opening of the Pacific World* tells the improbable story of how bat excrement led to an agricultural revolution. For more detail on the runaway population growth of chickens, see Jerry Adler and Andrew Lawler's essay, "How the Chicken Conquered the World." William Foege's memoir, *House on Fire*, supplies a first-person account of the eradication of smallpox.

NOTES

The Speckled Monster (Vaccines)

"set of old women": Quoted in Carrell, *The Speckled Monster*, 73.

"The boy was . . .": Quoted in Carrell, *The Speckled Monster*, 82.

The Detectives (Public Health Data)

"You and I may . . .": Quoted in Rawnsley, *Henry Whitehead*, 206.

Mapping the Seventh Ward (Social Epidemiology)

"The problem lay . . .": Du Bois, *The Philadelphia Negro*, 36.

"The mass of Negroes . . .": Du Bois, *The Philadelphia Negro*, 328.

Safe as Milk (Pasteurization)

"The reckless use of . . .": Straus, *Disease in Milk*, 98.

"Pasteurization prevents much . . .": Straus, *Disease in Milk*, 286.

Beyond the Placebo Effect (Drug Testing and Regulation)

All quotes from Frances Oldham Kelsey: "Autobiographical Reflections,"
fda.gov/media/89162/download

"The existing Food and Drugs Act . . .": Quoted in West, "The Accidental
Poison That Founded the Modern FDA."

The Mold That Changed the World (Antibiotics)

"Desperately and pathetically ill": Quoted in Lax, *The Mold in Dr. Florey's Coat*, 186.

"Florey [was] reserved and . . .": Quoted in Lax, *The Mold in Dr. Florey's Coat*, 190.

"Patient A: eye drops . . .": Wainwright, "Hitler's Penicillin," 189–198.

The Rocket Sled (Automobile Safety)

"The utmost gloom . . .": Quoted in "The World's First Fatal Car Accident—31 August 1869."

"I felt a sensation . . .": Quoted in Ryan, *Sonic Wind*, 107.

Conclusion: The Work Left to Do

"Medicine has never . . .": Jefferson to Jenner, letter.

"If we were smallpox . . .": Foege, *House on Fire*, 76.

"the world and all its peoples . . .": quoted in Henderson, 884.

"Of all the forms . . .": King, press conference.

BIBLIOGRAPHY

Adler, Jerry. "How the Chicken Conquered the World," *Smithsonian Magazine*, June 2012, 2012. www.smithsonianmag.com/history/how-the-chicken-conquered-the-world -87583657/#IfRbIAss4zRjbFBE.99.

Ballentine, Carol. "Taste of Raspberries, Taste of Death: The 1937 Elixir Sulfanilamide Incident." *FDA Consumer*, June 1981.

Barry, John M. *The Great Influenza: The Story of the Deadliest Pandemic in History.* New York: Penguin Books, 2018.

Bendiner, Elmer. "Alexander Fleming: Player with Microbes." *Hospital Practice* 24, no. 2 (1989), 283–316. doi:10.1080/21548331.1989.117 03671.

Bloom, David E., et al. "The Value of Vaccination." In *Fighting the Diseases of Poverty*, edited by Philip Stevens, 214–38. New York: Routledge, 2017.

Borroz, Tony. "Strapping Success: The 3-Point Seatbelt Turns 50." *Wired*, August 13, 2009. www.wired.com/2009/08/strapping-success-the-3-point-seatbelt-turns-50.

Bulletin of the World Health Organization. "Miracle Cure for an Old Scourge. An Interview with Dr. Dhiman Barua." 2009, www.readcube.com/articles /10.2471%2Fblt.09.050209

Carrell, Jennifer Lee. *The Speckled Monster: A Historical Tale of Battling Smallpox.* New York: Plume, 2004.

Cohen, Mark Nathan. *Health and the Rise of Civilization.* New Haven, CT: Yale University Press, 2011.

Cushman, G. T. *Guano and the Opening of the Pacific World: A Global Ecological History.* Cambridge, UK: Cambridge University Press, 2013.

Deaton, Angus. *The Great Escape: Health, Wealth, and the Origins of Inequality.* Princeton, NJ: Princeton University Press, 2015.

DeHaven, Hugh. "Mechanical Analysis of Survival in Falls from Heights of Fifty to One Hundred and Fifty Feet." *Injury Prevention* 6, no. 1, (2000). doi:10.1136/ip.6.1.62-b.

Dillon, John J. *Seven Decades of Milk: A History of New York's Dairy Industry.* Ann Arbor,

MI: University of Michigan Press, 1993.

Du Bois, W. E. B. *The Philadelphia Negro (The Oxford W. E. B. Du Bois)*. New York: Oxford University Press, 2014.

Eyler, John M. *Victorian Social Medicine: The Ideas and Methods of William Farr*. Baltimore: Johns Hopkins University Press, 1979.

Farris, Chris. "Moldy Mary . . . Or a Simple Messenger Girl?" *Peoria Magazine*, December 2019. www.peoriamagazines.com/pm/2019/dec/moldy-mary-or-simple -messenger-girl.

Foege, William H. *House on Fire: The Fight to Eradicate Smallpox*. Oakland, CA: University of California Press, 2012.

Fogel, Robert. *The Escape from Hunger and Premature Death, 1700–2100*. New York: Cambridge University Press, 2003.

Friend, Tad. "Silicon Valley's Quest to Live Forever." *The New Yorker*, March 27, 2017. www.newyorker.com/magazine/2017/04/03/silicon-valleys-quest-to-live-forever.

Gawande, Atul. "Slow Ideas." *The New Yorker*, July 22, 2013. www.newyorker.com /magazine/2013/07/29/slow-ideas.

Henderson, Donald A. "A History of Eradication: Successes, Failures, and Controversies." *The Lancet* 379, no. 9,819 (2012): 884–5.

Hopkins, Donald R. *The Greatest Killer: Smallpox in History*. Chicago: University of Chicago Press, 2002.

Jefferson, Thomas. Letter from Jefferson to George C. Jenner, May 14, 1806. Library of Congress. https://www.loc.gov/resource/mtj1.036_0006_0006.

Johnson, Steven. *The Ghost Map: The Story of London's Most Terrifying Epidemic—and How It Changed Science, Cities, and the Modern World*. New York: Riverhead, 2006.

Kelsey, Frances Oldham. "Autobiographical Reflections." https://www.fda.gov /media/89162/download.

King Jr., Dr. Martin Luther. Press conference, March 25, 1966, before speech at the second convention of the Medical Committee for Human Rights. muse.jhu.edu /article/686948/pdf.

Lax, Eric. *The Mold in Dr. Florey's Coat: The Story of the Penicillin Miracle*. New York: Henry Holt, 2005.

Lewis, David L. *W. E. B. Du Bois: A Biography, 1868–1963*. New York: Henry Holt and Company, 2009.

McGuire, Michael J. *The Chlorine Revolution: The History of Water Disinfection and the Fight to Save Lives*. Denver: Water Works Association, 2013.

Moss, Tyler. "The 19th-Century Swill Milk Scandal That Poisoned Infants with Whiskey Runoff." Atlas Obscura, November 27, 2017. www.atlasobscura.com/articles/swill-milk

-scandal-new-york-city.

Nader, Ralph. *Unsafe at Any Speed: The Designed-In Dangers of the American Automobile.* New York: Knightsbridge Publishing Co., 1991.

Nelson, Bryn. "The Lingering Heat over Pasteurized Milk." Science History Institute, April 1, 2009. www.sciencehistory.org/distillations/the-lingering-heat-over-pasteurized-milk.

Pinker, Steven. *Enlightenment Now: The Case for Reason, Science, Humanism, and Progress.* New York: Penguin Books, 2019.

Razzell, Peter Ernest. *The Conquest of Smallpox: The Impact of Inoculation on Smallpox Mortality in Eighteenth Century Britain.* London: Caliban Books, 2003.

Rawnsley, Hardwick D. *Henry Whitehead: A Memorial Sketch.* James MacLehose and Sons: Glasgow, 1898.

Riley, James C. *Rising Life Expectancy: A Global History.* New York: Cambridge University Press, 2015.

Rosen, William. *Miracle Cure: The Creation of Antibiotics and the Birth of Modern Medicine.* New York: Penguin Books, 2018.

Ryan, Craig. *Sonic Wind: The Story of John Paul Stapp and How a Renegade Doctor Became the Fastest Man on Earth.* New York: Liveright, 2016.

Straus, Nathan. *Disease in Milk: The Remedy Pasteurization: The Life Work of Nathan Straus.* Smithtown, NY: Straus Historical Society, Inc., 2016.

Wainwright, Milton. "Hitler's Penicillin." *Perspectives in Biology and Medicine* 47, no. 2 (2004): 189–198. doi:10.1353/pbm.2004.0037.

West, Julian G. "The Accidental Poison That Founded the Modern FDA." *The Atlantic,* January 16, 2018. www.theatlantic.com/technology/archive/2018/01/the-accidental-poison-that-founded-the-modern-fda/550574.

"The World's First Fatal Car Accident—31 August 1869," The British Newspaper Archive blog, August 30, 2013. blog.britishnewspaperarchive.co.uk/2013/08/30/worlds-first-fatal-car-accident/.

Zaimeche, Salah, and Salim Al-Hassani. "Lady Montagu and the Introduction of Smallpox Inoculation to England." *Muslim Heritage,* February 16, 2010. muslimheritage.com/lady-montagu-smallpox-inoculation-england.

INDEX

Page numbers in *italics* indicate photos

Food and Drug Administration (FDA) (formerly the Bureau of Chemistry), 44–53

G

Geiling, Eugene, 41–42, 44–45
guano, 84–85

H

Haber, Fritz, 85–86
Heatley, Norman, 59, *59*
Henderson, D. A., 94
Hill, Austin Bradford, 48
Hitler, Adolf, 65–67
Hunt, Mary ("Moldy Mary"), 62–63

I

illness outbreaks due to factory farming, 91
the immune system, 47
inequality, health, 99–100
inoculation. *See* variolation

J

Jefferson, Thomas, 93–94
Jenner, Edward, 7–8, 10–11, 12, 56, 93–94

K

Kelsey, Frances Oldham. *See* Oldham, Frances
Kennedy, John F., 51, *51*

L

life expectancy

W

PHOTO CREDITS